More Praise for *TouchPoints*

"In this day and age, it's easy to assume that all leadership concepts have been discovered and written about. Then along comes *TouchPoints*, with an idea as simple as it is powerful: interactions with people matter, and you can become a much better leader by taking advantage of these opportunities. I'm putting this to work Monday morning."
— Jon Spector, CEO, The Conference Board

"Tremendous! Conant and Norgaard have written a masterpiece on leadership. Simultaneously filled with profound wisdom and practical application, this book demonstrates how our moment-to-moment interactions with others are really opportunities to listen, learn, teach, and understand the pulse of our people and organization. This remarkable book will forever change how we view the work of leadership."
— Stephen M. R. Covey, Author of *The New York Times* and #1 *Wall Street Journal* best-selling book, *The Speed of Trust*

"Thinking about leadership as managing an ongoing series of TouchPoints is a fascinating concept. What you once considered to be interruptions will be appreciated as the serious stuff of business, to be managed and used every day."
— Shelly Lazarus, Chairman, Ogilvy & Mather Worldwide

"*TouchPoints* is a glorious gem of a book about the real work of leaders—the daily, in-the-moment, right-now actions that bring mastery to every interaction. Conant and Norgaard write with ease and elegance, presenting a powerful and positive message about how the smallest actions can have the biggest impact. *TouchPoints* is packed with practical tips on how you can use your head, hands, and heart to more fully engage those you lead. It's a book you'll want to savor, use, and reuse."
— Jim Kouzes, coauthor of the best-selling *The Leadership Challenge*; Dean's Executive Professor of Leadership, Leavey School of Business

"Walk every shift on the factory floor—you will learn more from that than what you read in the productivity reports. Make yourself available 24/7 and care about people, they are the business. This book is all about effective leadership, and effective leadership is what drives shareowner value and career progression. It's a read for all."
— Bill Perez, former President and CEO, Nike

"Some CEOs chafe at being held to account for the performance of vast pools of employees far from their immediate contact. *TouchPoints* closes the gap between leader initiative and empowered work groups by looking at how leaders can learn from team members, inform constituents of new directions, and inspire greatness by leveraging a rich portfolio of direct personal interventions throughout their enterprise. Doug and Mette draw upon their compelling firsthand experiences for vivid, persuasive demonstrations of just how to do it."

— Jeffrey Sonnenfeld,
Senior Associate Dean for Executive Programs,
Lester Crown Professor or Management Practice,
Yale School of Management

"*TouchPoints* is both simple and profound. How can you lead more effectively in the face of every day hurdles? By leaning into every encounter with new intention and skill. Equip yourself by reading this book."

— Anne Mulcahy, former Chairwoman
and CEO of Xerox

"Conant and Norgaard have captured the essence of great leadership by emphasizing the importance of what happens every day in both formal and informal interactions. All too often, leaders fall short of their potential because they focus more on time efficiency than personal impact. This book will convince you that the latter is what matters most—and can help you make it happen."

— Jon Katzenbach, Senior Partner,
Katzenbach Center at Booz & Company

"It is clear that the successful companies in East Asia are conscious of the ideas so clearly expressed in *TouchPoints*. Asian business leaders now have a book that they can give to the members of their organizations—particularly to those who will be taking over from the 'founders.'"

— Wash SyCip, Founder, SGV Group

"*TouchPoints* is a guide to bringing the humanity back into leadership and turning those constant interruptions into pockets of leadership development gold. It will help you become a better leader and a better person."

— Alvin Rohrs, President and CEO,
Students in Free Enterprise Worldwide (SIFE)

"The authors outline a masterful plan for conquering the hard work of leadership. Step by step, they reveal what it takes to remain connected to a true sense of purpose while facing the everyday struggle of leading."

— Alan Hassenfeld, Chairman of the
Executive Committee, Hasbro, Inc.

"*TouchPoints* is an outstanding primer on the keystone concepts of making leadership much more effective in any situation. Given today's nonstop pace, these techniques and concepts are in fact essential for anyone. A must-read for the top of every leader's list."

— Colonel Daniel K. Fetzer (USAF Retired), former Chief of
Nuclear, Biological and Chemical Warfare Defense for U.S.
CENTCOM under General Norman Schwarzkopf

"Effective leaders know how to blend technology and people to advance their organization's mission and impact. This book provides insightful counsel on mastering the art of the strategic human touch."

— Sally Blount, Dean, Kellogg School of Management
at Northwestern University

"*TouchPoints* has it right. Every interaction, every choice, no matter how small, is an opportunity to demonstrate leadership. From the board table to the kitchen table, true leadership is a 24/7 job."

— Marilyn Carlson Nelson, Chairman, Carlson;
author of *How We Lead Matters*

"Nowhere have I read a more compelling case for skill-building for seasoned and emerging leaders. Drawing on their own real-world experiences and lessons learned by others, Norgaard and Conant will inspire you to lead with more intention, confidence, and influence. I invite you to start mastering your touchpoints today—with that seemingly simple question, 'How can I help?'"

— Dr. Johnnetta Betsch Cole, President Emerita of Spelman
College and Bennett College for Women

"Doug Conant's deep understanding of business, leadership and people all come together in *TouchPoints*. With Mette Norgaard, he provides an excellent guide for driving results through the skilled use of personal interactions."

— James M. Kilts, former Chairman and CEO,
The Gillette Company

"This book carries a great message: Set high standards, and encourage your people to achieve those standards using a new connective, powerful approach. It all starts with the authors' seemingly small question, "How can I help?" Like me, you'll find that when you ask it, you'll get more information, more useful problem solving, and more personal rewards. Let there be more touchpoints, and leaders who touchpoint!"

— Henrietta Holsman Fore,
former Administrator of United States
Agency for International Development (USAID)

"*TouchPoints* treats the intersection between leadership and interactions in a new, innovative way. Throughout his impressive career, Doug Conant has driven results and culture by adhering to a set of core values. He and Mette Norgaard offer an impatient call to action and lessons to learn for all leaders and aspiring leaders"

— Charles H. Moore, Executive Director,
Committee Encouraging Corporate Philanthropy

"Great books on leadership can be inspirational or instructive in a highly practical way. *TouchPoints* is both, and enormously entertaining to boot. If you aspire to have a highly positive impact on any kind of organization, you must buy this book."

— Jeffrey E. Garten, Professor and former Dean,
Yale School of Management

"*TouchPoints* is a vivid reminder that leadership is a 24/7 role. Every human contact is an opportunity for leadership. This book is required reading for current and aspiring leaders. It will make you rethink how to approach the most demanding role of the CEO."

—Carlos Gutierrez, former Secretary of Commerce;
former Chairman and CEO, Kellogg Company

"Leadership at the top is tough, and getting it right really matters. Every leader today struggles with the question, 'How can I have more impact in the midst of increasing demands and uncertainties?' As Conant and Norgaard know, you do it by managing your touchpoints well—moment upon moment, day upon day. Everyone who aspires to great and sustainable performance must master this discipline."

— Saj-nicole Joni, confidential CEO advisor;
author of *The Right Fight*

"There are few opinions in the world I trust more than Doug Conant's on the subject of real human development of colleagues. He and co-author Mette Norgaard have delivered an inspired book that will aid in your personal success."

— Jim Clifton, Chairman and CEO, Gallup

"Conant and Norgaard speak from the heart with passion and truth. *TouchPoints* can guide you on your first day on a new job and at the moment when you are made CEO. It's about magic in every inter-action. It's about how to create motivation, provide guidance, marshall wisdom, and drive progress."

— Michael Silverstein, Senior Partner and Managing Director, The Boston Consulting Group

"Doug and Mette's combination of leadership experience, real-life sto-ries, and thoughtful insights make their book a real asset for leaders anywhere."

— Brian Walker, CEO, Herman Miller

"Doug Conant is famous in the consumer food industry for transforming struggling companies like Nabisco and Campbell Soup into high func-tioning, high potential organizations. *TouchPoints*, which details Conant and Norgaard's strategy of viewing daily interruptions as a leader's oppor-tunity to influence, inspire, and shape events, is a must-read for new and seasoned executives alike."

— Alexandra Levit, syndicated business columnist; author of *New Job, New You*

"Executives lead by example and their organizations watch what they do to see if their behavior is consistent with their words. Conant and Norgaard show how interactions with people can be effective leadership moments. Well worth reading from two outstanding people."

— Harvey Golub, retired chairman and CEO, American Express

"In *TouchPoints*, Norgaard and Conant capture the essence of leadership. I have watched Doug Conant at work for a decade—he laid out his vision, strategies and plans, and he delivered exactly what it said on the Campbell's can. I thought this was because he was a natural leader (he is), but it's more intentional than that. He has figured out how to leverage every moment, every touchpoint, to make an enterprise soar."

— Andrew Robertson, President & CEO, BBDO Worldwide, Inc.

"You have about 1,672 TouchPoint opportunities per day. I If you seize just three magical moments in the way that Conant and Norgaard detail in this book, you'll cause an exciting, positive change in your life, your family's life, *and* your company's future."

— Debra Benton, author of *CEO Material:*
How to Be a Leader in Any Organization

"Today's tech-driven world works at warp speed. How do some leaders still manage to move their agenda forward, when others barrel through their days but seem to go nowhere? This powerful new book lays out what we all can do to spend our 'moments capital' more wisely. Bottom line is, if you want more impact, today and forever, master your TouchPoints."

— Charlene Li, best-selling author of
Groundswell and *Open Leadership*

"*TouchPoints* rightly reminds us that EVERY single interaction is the real work of leaders and the opportunity to raise performance now and next time."

— Greg Page, CEO, Cargill Inc.

"*TouchPoints* captures the art and science of leading in the moment. It teaches practical lessons about discovering the tremendous value that's right there in front of us, every day, in our basic human connections. Norgaard and Conant show leaders at all levels how to unleash the power of relationships to make good things happen in our super-saturated, interruptible world."

— Stew Friedman, Practice Professor, The Wharton School;
author of the best-selling *Total Leadership:*
Be a Better Leader, Have a Richer Life

"Conant and Norgaard have it right: leadership is a daily practice. It comes from an ongoing commitment to people and to making every interaction count. Through its powerful stories and recommendations, *TouchPoints* shows how you can become a more effective, valued leader."

— Sloan Gibson, President and CEO, USO

"Conant and Norgaard deliver fresh, clear-eyed advice on how you can start to deepen the commitment and performance of others, with one simple question to those around you. Remarkably actionable, *TouchPoints* deserves to be read by every member of the organization from the most senior leaders to frontline personnel. It's must reading for yourself and your team today."

— Michael Beer, Cahners-Rabb Professor of
Business Administration, Emeritus, at the Harvard
Business School; Chairman of TruePoint

"Doug and Mette help us rediscover the missed opportunities for leadership found in the hustle and bustle of our everyday business lives. They provide insight into how to recognize these everyday moments and use them to inspire deeper engagement, reinforce company values, and move a strategy forward. *TouchPoints* will be useful for all business leaders."

— Dave Dillon, Chairman and CEO,
The Kroger Company

"Doug and Mette believe that if people are the engine of our success, we need to touch our people's hearts every day. *TouchPoints* is an inspiring, thoughtful, and engaging reminder that leaders are in the people business—the business of motivating people to deliver results."

— Charles P. Garcia, best-selling author of *Leadership
Lessons of the White House Fellows*

"Conant and Norgaard have brought you good news: proven strategies for engaging your talent by unlocking the power of hundreds of latent leadership moments."

— Jane Hyun, executive coach, global leadership strategist,
and author of *Breaking the Bamboo Ceiling*

"In this bold new book, Conant and Norgaard lay out the strategies and tactics that we all must adopt to accommodate the forces around us and advance our agendas. I strongly recommend *TouchPoints* as your personal guidebook for effective leadership today."

— Pamela Bailey, President and CEO,
Grocery Manufacturers Association

"An essential read, *TouchPoints* will teach you how to transform everyday interactions and interruptions into opportunities to lead. Proven leaders in the business world, Conant and Norgaard reveal how you can take advantage of every moment—no matter how small—to assert influence and lead more effectively."

— Ilene H. Lang, President &
Chief Executive Officer, Catalyst

"I am in firm belief that we are on the verge of the humanization of business and brands, and what Doug and Mette are pointing to is an extremely important message to all leaders who will be executing in this new economy. If you are running a company today or thinking of ever running one, please read this book."

> — Gary Vaynerchuck, Cofounder of VaynerMedia;
> author of *The Thank You Economy*

"In today's fast-moving world, opportunities to make a difference can pass us by. Norgaard and Conant provide a powerful TouchPoints strategy to all of us who strive to transform daily interactions into opportunities for great leadership moments and meaningful connections with others."

> —Sara Mathew, Chairman & CEO, D&B

"Leadership, in any circumstance, is about making change happen. *TouchPoints* shows how do to this more effectively by simply leveraging your interactions with others, one by one. Do yourself a favor and read this powerful book."

> — Chris Gardner, business leader, philanthropist,
> and author of *Pursuit of Happyness*

"Conant and Norgaard offer a fresh and enduring way to move forward with greater impact, starting with your next one-on-one encounter. *TouchPoints* opened my eyes to the potential for everyone to be a more accessible and action-oriented leader. This book will become required reading for my leadership team."

> — Barry Rand, CEO, AARP

"In *TouchPoints*, Campbell Soup's extraordinary CEO Doug Conant and Mette Norgaard have created a superb leadership guide to empower people by leading in every interaction—up close and personal, hands on, and tough-minded, yet tender-hearted. You'll learn an enormous amount about leadership if you let them mentor you through this remarkable book."

> — Bill George, Professor, Harvard Business School;
> author of *True North*

TouchPoints

Warren Bennis

A WARREN BENNIS BOOK

This collection of books is devoted exclusively to new and exemplary contributions to management thought and practice. The books in this series are addressed to thoughtful leaders, executives, and managers of all organizations who are struggling with and committed to responsible change. My hope and goal is to spark new intellectual capital by sharing ideas positioned at an angle to conventional thought—in short, to publish books that disturb the present in the service of a better future.

Books in the Warren Bennis Signature Series

TouchPoints

CREATING POWERFUL LEADERSHIP
CONNECTIONS IN THE SMALLEST
OF MOMENTS

Douglas R. Conant
Mette Norgaard

JOSSEY-BASS
A Wiley Imprint
www.josseybass.com

Published by Jossey-Bass
A Wiley Imprint
989 Market Street, San Francisco, CA 94103-1741—www.josseybass.com

Jossey-Bass books and products are available through most bookstores. To contact Jossey-Bass directly call our Customer Care Department within the U.S. at 800-956-7739, outside the U.S. at 317-572-3986, or fax 317-572-4002.

Jossey-Bass also publishes its books in a variety of electronic formats. Some content that appears in print may not be available in electronic books.

Library of Congress Cataloging-in-Publication Data

Conant, Douglas R., 1951-
  TouchPoints : creating powerful leadership connections in the smallest of moments / Douglas R. Conant, Mette Norgaard.
      p. cm. – (Warren Bennis series ; 169)
  Includes index.
  ISBN 978-1-118-00435-7; 978-1-118-07548-7 (ebk); 978-1-118-07550-0 (ebk); 978-1-118-07554-8 (ebk)
1. Leadership. I. Norgaard, Mette. II. Title.
  HD57.7.C649 2011
  658.4'092–dc22

                                                                    2011008907

Printed in the United States of America
FIRST EDITION
HB Printing   10 9 8 7 6 5 4 3 2 1

Contents

Contents

Editor's Note

It seems all too rare these days to encounter a leader who is able to fulfill his or her role in the truest sense of the word—to be both "tough-minded and tender-hearted" as Doug Conant and Mette Norgaard describe in this extraordinary book. And yet I know they are out there—and what is more, there are many, many others who, if they had the example, the inspiration, and the instruction, could master a leadership approach that is at once flexible, easy to understand, and, most important, effective.

Doug Conant, a "leader of leaders," is the CEO of the Campbell Soup Company—a universally known brand that has encountered the same challenges of any large company of late; Mette Norgaard, a "teacher of leaders," has been instrumental working with Doug and the larger leadership group at Campbell and in her own consulting beyond. They have come together to produce a book that unpacks the very essence of what a true leader does day in and day out: with intention, he or she moves things forward in a series of interactions that are made up of moments. This notion is at once simple and profound, for when you think about how many instances are available to one who is willing to pay attention, who is willing to become self-aware, who is willing to simply say, "How can I help?" you realize the enormity of the opportunity—as well as the enormity of the effort. For though it may be "simple," it is not easy. It requires a deep sense of humanity; of doing what it is right; of commitment; of daily, weekly, monthly, and yearly *practice*. What I love about the authors' TouchPoints approach is that it makes clear sense, and it is proven! It points out that there are spaces in between where something is and what something might become—and that these moments are ours to seize. If we lead with this notion in mind, we have broken leadership down to its essence.

How to go about it effectively is the next obvious question—and here the authors can expertly guide you. Doug's own experiences over the past ten years at Campbell are a virtual laboratory of how the TouchPoints approach, bit by bit, has made a clear impact. His stories here are priceless. Mette's work with leaders of all stripes is also here, and shows us how various people in different professions around the world have successfully put the approach to use.

As someone who continues to think about, write about, and learn about leadership, I was moved by this book. It reminds us that "leadership is not about *you*—it is about *them*," and that leadership is both incredibly soft and unceasingly hard. Ultimately, it helps us understand how to open up the space that is needed to really advance issues. Yes, it is incredible work we commit to—to do it well and to do it to the best of our ability is likely the most challenging effort we can undertake. And the genius is that we will always have another opportunity to grow it and learn it, if we commit to it. Remember, these authors say, if you forget where to start, you can simply ask "How can I help?"

Warren Bennis
Santa Monica, California
February 2011

Foreword

*L*eadership encompasses many things, and the "work" of a leader at any level in an organization demands a certain kind of self-awareness and focused attention. It is important that the leader understands—probably more than anything else—what needs to happen to move an issue forward. Yet many of the leaders I have encountered do not get the very basics—that the "interruptions" of their day, both planned and unplanned, give them an opportunity to get in there and really lead. Doug Conant and Mette Norgaard *do* get this, and they have distilled a tested approach that makes the most of these moments. They direct the leader in three key steps: first, to listen closely to understand an issue; second, having gained that understanding, to help frame the actual situation; and third, to advance the conversation in order to advance the issue. This "listen, frame, advance" TouchPoints triad they share here is something that anyone can put into practice and see results from.

I have worked with leaders of all stripes, and what I like most about the TouchPoints approach is that it works—it is not some esoteric academic theory. Doug has been modeling this approach since he began at Campbell, and it has reaped deep results—and helped create a world-class company that knows how to grow its own leaders from the inside. This bench strength is without a doubt the most important thing a CEO can develop; this pool of leaders models the behavior for others, and it becomes a very part of the company fabric. If embedded right, it has the potential to turn what might be a mediocre organization into something extraordinary. But as anyone knows who has tried it, it is not simply a switch you turn on—it demands that a leader step up and put it to use. There are likely to be many stumbles along the way, but that is where this book will come in handy and become invaluable.

I have known Doug and Mette for many years. I have had the good fortune of seeing them work up close, and what they have accomplished together is unusual. They are a true intellectual team: each one's strengths complement the other's, and they are to be commended for their work on developing these ideas over the last five years into something that a wide audience can benefit from. Many (many!) years ago, I had the good fortune of being Doug's teacher in graduate school. He was, and continues to be, an eager and thoughtful student of what works and has real impact. I find myself the student now—learning from a practitioner who has been up and down quite a few mountains. It is clear to me that his and Mette's contribution with this book will do more than help others simply "do better." *TouchPoints* advances the leadership conversation greatly. And for that, we should all be grateful.

Ram Charan
February 2011

Preface

When Doug took over as CEO of Campbell in 2001, the company's stock was trailing the S&P 500 and falling precipitously, the core businesses were in disrepair, the organization was in shambles, and Campbell was the poorest performer of all the major food companies in the world. Doug's job as the new CEO was to stop the bleeding, stabilize the situation, and get the company back on its feet.

It wouldn't be easy. Employees were shell-shocked by the battering they were experiencing on all fronts. For almost everyone, including Doug, this meant difficult daily encounters—with a disillusioned consumer, an irate customer, a frustrated coworker, an indifferent supplier   that were always challenging and often unpleasant. To make matters worse, the systems for managing all those situations were largely dysfunctional. People felt tired, unappreciated, and like victims of their circumstances.

But Doug had come to Campbell with a reputation for engineering turnarounds in the food industry. As president of the Nabisco Food Company, he had taken a large division from mediocrity to delivering five consecutive years of sales, earnings, and market share growth. How had he done it? He rebuilt the company with a philosophy of being tough-minded on the standards and tender-hearted with the people. "Some joked that my approach was a cross between Pollyanna and Don Quixote," Doug says, "but I have no apologies. The people were highly engaged and delivering excellent results. We grew earnings at a double-digit rate for five straight years. If that's a sign of weakness, I'll take it every time."

Could he do it again at Campbell?

The answer was a resounding "Yes!" By 2009, the company was outperforming both the S&P Food Group and the S&P 500. Sales and earnings were growing, the core businesses were thriving, the employees were highly engaged in their work, the company was increasingly being recognized for its progress with workforce diversity and inclusion, and Campbell was ranked as one of the ten most socially responsible U.S. companies. Doug and his team had achieved something extraordinary.

They advanced their vision for Campbell by using positive sequences of interactions focused within a winning strategic framework to tangibly demonstrate to the employees that they cared; tough sequences to establish world-class standards; and teaching sequences to develop the leaders around them. It was only later, while the two of us, Mette and Doug, were working on this book, that we came up with the term *TouchPoints* to describe the interactions that Doug, his team, and, ultimately, twenty thousand associates used to help turn Campbell around.

WHY THIS BOOK

Leadership is tough. As a leader, you must constantly meet and exceed targets. To perform consistently, you have to be prepared to make decisions and mobilize others *right now*. There is never enough time: there are customer issues, board issues, vendor issues, employee issues. The phone system malfunctions, the production line goes down, the PDA stops working, you have to fill in for someone at the last minute, and you are always on the road. It's an everyday struggle. The pace is fast and furious, the accountabilities are in real time, and one thoughtless action can be posted on YouTube and make its way around the world before the day is over. How can you manage to get *anything* done in an environment where you are lucky if you can average four minutes of uninterrupted time in a day?

That was a question we posed to each other one morning when we were a world away from such frenetic activity, strolling the grounds at Skytop Lodge in the Pocono Mountains. It was the last day of a Campbell

CEO Institute retreat, a two-year development program for a select number of Campbell's high-potential leaders.

We had met years before, while Doug was at Nabisco and Mette was leading the executive development program for the Covey Leadership Center in Utah. We reconnected again when Mette was interviewing Doug for a book she was writing on leadership, which led to our collaboration on the CEO Institute.

That morning in the Poconos, we were still feeling the contemplative energy from the previous night's bonfire, where the Institute's participants had sat in silence, reflecting on their personal leadership philosophy and capturing their insights in their journals. Knowing we would soon have to leave the peaceful Poconos and return to the "real" world, Mette asked Doug, "Don't you get tired of the ceaseless interruptions?"

After a moment of thought, Doug said, "To me, they're not interruptions. They're opportunities to touch someone and improve the situation." Whereas most people kept trying to minimize the dozens and dozens of encounters they experience every day at work, he believed that those encounters *were* the work, and that how he handled them would ultimately define his success as a contributor and as a leader.

As the two of us headed back to the group, we began to talk about whether the leadership perspective that had been so successful at Nabisco and at Campbell might be useful to others. What might happen, we asked ourselves, if leaders could stop swatting at urgencies and interruptions as if they were pesky mosquitoes, and instead use them as opportunities to influence? What if real leadership could take place in the hundreds of interactions that made up a leader's day? Then, because it is not possible to predict what each moment might bring, leaders would need to be extremely well prepared. And to prepare themselves, they would have to reflect on the vital leadership questions that Mette was currently writing about and that we were teaching at the CEO Institute. This conversation led to our writing this book together.

During the next four years, we probed the nature of a leader's scheduled and spontaneous interactions, drawing on our combined experience—Doug's as a leader of leaders and Mette's as a teacher of leaders—to understand what it takes for a leader to stand in the stream of such moments and influence their direction. As our concept took shape, we came up with the name TouchPoints to describe the way that each of the many interactions leaders have with others during their workday gives them the chance to "touch" someone: to influence, guide, provide clarity, inspire, create a sense of urgency, and shape the course of events. We've now spent countless hours exploring, discussing, and trying out the TouchPoints concept with a wide range of leaders from all over the world. It's an approach that works!

TouchPoint leadership is not about running faster, working longer, and wringing more productivity out of every waking minute. It's about being present in the moment and feeling confident that you can deal with whatever happens in a way that is helpful to others—and by extension, to yourself and your organization. Touch-Points do not replace the leadership models that work for you. Instead, they infuse them with energy. They offer a way of working that is ideally suited to the vagaries and demands of today's organizations.

ABOUT THIS BOOK

Why are you reading this book? Are you an experienced leader looking for ideas that can help you get better at your job? New to leadership and seeking advice on how to become the best leader you can be? Aspiring to a leadership position and curious about what being a leader really means? No matter what your current position or your purpose, you'll find that the ideas in these pages will help you prepare yourself to work more effectively and efficiently in the interruption age. They will help you lead in the smallest of moments.

In the first chapter we explain what TouchPoints are all about, and in the second we discuss the commitment to TouchPoint mastery. In the last four chapters you'll find practical information and ideas that you can use right away, in your very next interaction, and to continue developing as a leader. In each chapter you'll find real stories from real leaders that illustrate the power of TouchPoints.

Reflecting on and learning from experience is critical to success for anyone, especially leaders, whose decisions and actions can affect so many people and have such significant consequences. Throughout the book, we've included a number of questions to help you think about these concepts as they apply to your own situation.

We encourage you to use the ideas and questions in the book to develop your capabilities as you aim for mastery. Then, with each interaction, you will become better and better at leading in the moment. Over time, the cumulative impact of such interactions adds up to real change. They can turn around a project, a team—even a Fortune 500 company.

So let's get started.

TouchPoints

1

The Power of TouchPoints

THE ACTION IS IN THE INTERACTION

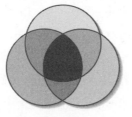

It's nearly three-thirty in the afternoon. You're holed up in your office, trying to grab some time to finish a proposal that's critical to the future of your department—and your own career—when a team member knocks on your door to ask for advice with a tricky problem. How do you respond? Do you give in to the flash of irritation you feel at being interrupted and tell him to come back later? Or do you stop what you are doing and help him right now? It's your choice.

As a leader, you make those choices all day, every day. The "knock on the door" happens over and over again—phone calls, meetings, emails, and text messages, all with questions to answer, concerns to address, problems to solve, and fires to put out. There are big issues and small issues, planned sessions and surprises, and they come at you constantly and from every direction. You have to make decisions without having all the information, and you need to make them *now*. The workload is expanding, and the time you have to deal with each issue is shrinking. Some days it feels as though the information age has morphed into the interruption age.

But what if you could step back and look at all those interactions with a fresh perspective? What if, instead of seeing them as interfering with your work, you were to look at them as latent leadership moments? What if these moments were the answer to leadership in today's busy world?

In our experience, that is precisely what they are. Each of the many connections you make has the potential to become a high point or a low point in someone's day. Each is an opportunity to establish high performance expectations, to infuse the agenda with greater clarity and more energy, and to influence the course of events. Each is a chance to transform an ordinary moment into a TouchPoint.

TouchPoints take place any time two or more people get together to deal with an issue and get something done. A casual conversation with a colleague becomes a TouchPoint when the focus shifts to an impending contract. An email exchange with a team member turns into a TouchPoint when she tells you about a production delay. The chit-chat before an afternoon meeting shifts to TouchPoint mode when the last person arrives and someone says, "Everyone's here—let's get started."

In fact, each day is an elaborate sequence of Touch-Points: interactions—with one other person, a couple of people, or a group—that can last a couple of minutes, a couple of hours, or a couple of days. Those TouchPoints can be planned or spontaneous, casual or carefully choreographed. They take place in hallways, on factory floors, in conference rooms, on the phone, and via email or instant messaging. Some deal with straightforward, relatively minor issues; others involve complex challenges with wide-ranging effects.

Sadly, leaders often see these interactions as distractions that get in the way of their real work: the important work of strategizing, planning, and prioritizing. But in our experience, these TouchPoints *are* the real work. They are the moments that bring your strategies and priorities to life, the interactions that translate your ideas into new and better behaviors. That is, providing you take these Touch-Points, no matter how brief, and infuse them with greater clarity and genuine commitment.

THREE VARIABLES, ONE TOUCHPOINT

Although there are many ways in which TouchPoints differ, they all have the same three variables: the issue, the other people, and the leader.

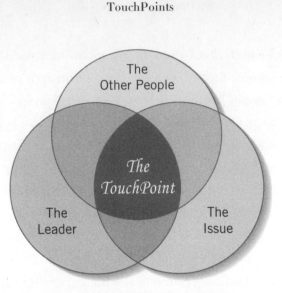

The Three Variables of a TouchPoint

The issue is something important, such as a question, a problem, or a decision that affects the performance of individuals, teams, units, or the entire organization. Such issues come at you fast and furiously from every direction. In many cases you have to make a decision quickly, even without having all the necessary information.

The issue could be how to address a customer complaint, cross-train employees, reschedule a meeting so that the right people can be there, find resources for a project after the budget has been cut, or replace a key team member who has suddenly resigned. The issue may even be building a relationship. In fact, many leaders initiate a large number of brief interactions whose sole purpose is to make positive connections so that when the leader needs to make a tough call, people will know they are valued and will trust the leader's intentions.

The other people are the stakeholders who are involved in the issue. In this book we will focus on internal stakeholders, such as the individuals who report to you directly and indirectly, your colleagues, and the people with whom you have a straight or dotted reporting line.

In today's interdisciplinary and international workplaces, these stakeholders may have diverse norms and values, which means they often make differing assumptions about what it means to be on time, deliver quality, show respect, and be loyal. Consequently, you need to be tuned in, because the behaviors that turn one person on may turn someone else off completely.

The leader is the person who brings a little magic to the moment. Taking the lead in a TouchPoint is not a matter of title or position; it is a matter of behavior. The leader is the one who listens carefully, helps others frame the issue, brings a sense of urgency, and creates confidence about the next step. When you are the most senior person in the room, that responsibility will be yours. In many situations, however, you may want to use that moment as an opportunity to guide and develop others.

To take the lead in a TouchPoint requires dual vision. That is, you need to be able to address the most pressing need and do it in a way that makes the others more capable, ready to take on the next issue. In other words, you must zero in on the needs of the *now*, while being mindful of the *next time*.

MY ISSUE, YOUR ISSUE, OR OUR ISSUE

Of course not every issue is your direct responsibility. That is why one of the first things you listen for in a TouchPoint is whether the issue at hand is "my issue," "your issue," or "our issue." If you own it, you can make the calls. If they own it, you want to help them make the best possible decision and be ready to move forward. If it is "ours," you share the responsibility with the other people.

When You Own the Issue

David has a visceral appreciation for the power of Touch-Points. When he was a plant manager for P&G, running sites with five hundred to a thousand people, he made it a habit to walk through the plant every day. In the course of a week, he would make sure he spent time with each of the four shifts. Among other things, he used his walk-throughs to deal with several of his own issues.

"I would routinely walk through the plant and connect with fifty to a hundred people in an hour. I always had a little slip of paper in my pocket with ten or twelve to-dos I needed to handle. They could range from getting an update on a safety issue to telling people about an award we had won." In David's experience, the biggest mistake plant managers make is that when they get really, really busy, they stop doing these kinds of tours. They think they can get more done by staying at their desk. But the exact opposite happens. "Walking the plant," David says, "you get so much done in a minute. You get little updates, you feel the pulse, you quietly reinforce the standards when you pick up a piece of trash and remind someone about ear protection. If people are busy, you just wave."

The walkabouts not only gave David a chance to deal with his issues but also served as opportunities for people to bring up their own. One person might walk along for a few yards to tell him that someone's husband was in the hospital; another might stop him to discuss a concern. In this way, his tours would shift from dealing with his own issues to helping other people with theirs.

The merit of such walkabouts is that they create dozens of proactive TouchPoints. By being ahead on the issues, making yourself available, and setting the tone, you anticipate and prevent a number of problems. By making time for interactions, you can prevent unnecessary interruptions.

When Someone Else Owns the Issue

When a direct report owns the issue, the challenge for many leaders is to leave the responsibility where it belongs. This is particularly difficult for leaders who were promoted because others trust them to get the job done. That was Nancy's challenge. In her previous position as the head of a national accounts team, she had always been the go-to person. When the customer had a problem, she would do everything she could to fix it, and fix it fast! She would ignore the chains of command and go directly to the person who could get the job done.

The problem was that, having been promoted to VP, Nancy was now going around her own people. She kept forgetting that as a leader of leaders, it was no longer her job to fix the problem directly. Her role now was to help others figure out how to deal with it.

To curb her impatience, Nancy developed a small TouchPoint habit. When her team was addressing a problem, she would first go around the room and hear from each team member what he or she thought should be done. Only at the end would she add her two cents' worth. "It was really hard at first. I felt I was inadequate because I wasn't *doing* something. But it was also fulfilling, because soon I began to see people step up in ways they had not done before. Today, it's exciting to see how each individual is so much stronger. In fact, the whole team is becoming really impressive."

What Nancy learned was that it is not enough to get the job done *now*. As a leader, you need to get the job done in a way that builds the individual's and team's capacity to do even better *next time*.

When You Share the Issue with Others

At other times, the leader and the other people are jointly responsible for the issue. That was the case when Jerry, a senior VP for public affairs, needed to bring Kim, a new director, up to speed.

Kim's role would be to lead an initiative to reduce childhood obesity and hunger in Camden, New Jersey, by 50 percent in ten years. "One Friday I took Kim and three other members of my team on a three-hour tour of the city," Jerry said, "and we visited our partners at a day-care center, an elementary school, and a community garden. It was a really good morning. Most important, it gave her an affirmation that what we are trying to do is needed and doable."

Bringing Kim up to speed was an issue that Kim and Jerry shared. By taking her on the tour, Jerry provided her with both a physical understanding of the city and a strong beginning to the relationships, which would help her get a head start on her new job.

THE POTENTIAL OF A TOUCHPOINT

Every TouchPoint is spring-loaded with possibilities. Each one can build—or break—a relationship. Even a brief interaction can change the way people think about themselves, their leaders, and their future.

Doug had such an experience that has stayed with him to this day. When he was in graduate school, he had a professor who had extremely high standards. One day, after Doug had handed in a carelessly done assignment, the professor called him in and said, simply, "Doug, you can do better."

"That's all he said," Doug recalls, "'You can do better,' and of course he was right. Moreover, he never needed to say it again." Now when Doug reviews work that doesn't meet his standards, instead of giving people negative feedback, he challenges them to do better in some specific way. As it did with Doug, the statement "You can do better" often goes a long way toward increasing people's confidence and encouraging them to stretch.

Mette, in contrast, remembers an experience of her own that shows the negative potential of TouchPoints. It happened when she was product manager for a mid-size multinational company. After discovering that a new product was failing to meet the company's quality criteria, she recommended to her immediate boss, the director of marketing, that they stop production until they figured out what the problem was.

When Mette's boss took the issue to the vice president, however, he was told in no uncertain terms, "This is the fourth quarter. You've got to keep the line moving so we can make the numbers." After that meeting, Mette's boss called her into his office and told her that her job was to keep the line moving at all costs. When Mette protested, he snapped at her, "If you can't do it, I'll find a real man for the job."

Mette's boss got the job done—the production line kept moving—but he lost her respect. What was worse, she also lost respect for herself. She thought her superiors were making the wrong call and wished she had shown more backbone. This experience shows that when a leader goes for compliance instead of commitment, he may erode a person's confidence and damage the relationship.

Have you had these kinds of experiences—positive TouchPoints that increased your confidence and commitment, or negative interactions that left you feeling worse about others or yourself? If so, you already know the power and possibilities of a moment. You know the potential of a TouchPoint.

TouchPoints can inspire people to give the very best of themselves, and they can cause people to shut down. Like money, TouchPoints in and of themselves are neither good nor bad. What matters is how you use them. They are a resource that you can either invest or squander.

Like Doug's professor, we all have times when we say just the right thing. Like Mette's boss, we also have times when we botch it.

That's a fact of life. What is important is that you continuously strive to increase your ratio of "That went well!" to "I blew it." If you reflect on the TouchPoints you've engaged in during the past few weeks, what is your ratio? What would you like it to be?

It's important to remember that improving that ratio is not about becoming nicer; it is about becoming more effective. It is about engaging people and moving forward faster, instead of tripping up and slowing down. It is about gaining commitment instead of settling for compliance.

Whether you are a manager, a mentor, or a parent, you want to touch others in a way that makes them *want* to do the right thing. You want to guide them in a way that helps them make good decisions, even when you are not in the room—which, if you are a leader of leaders, is 99.9 percent of the time.

THE EXPONENTIAL EFFECT OF A TOUCHPOINT

TouchPoint leadership capitalizes on the social networking effect, what we call the *exponential effect*.

Every person you engage with is embedded in webs of relationships. Whatever you say or do in a TouchPoint may be quickly transmitted to five or six people in that person's network—and then relayed to their colleagues, and so on. Therefore, when you impart a sense of urgency, people may pass that on; when you inspire confidence, that too may be transmitted; and when you blow it, everyone is bound to hear about it.

George, head of an R&D department with five hundred people, recalls a recent TouchPoint that illustrates the exponential effect. "It was one of those very contentious meetings with the senior executives where people were debating a specific and rather narrow point," he explained. After listening intently for a while, he realized that the issue had been framed too narrowly. Though George was not the most senior person in the room, "I found myself articulating the broader strategic view, one where R&D had the right to make certain decisions. It was a very lonely point of view, yet I advocated it quite passionately."

Later that day, George ran into a colleague from the legal department, and he was surprised to hear that she knew about his argument. How? It turned out that his team members were excited that he had taken such a strong stand, felt proud of the way he had represented the department, and had spread the word. "When we are leaders," George said, "others are watching everything we do. The issue I raised was of great importance to our team. Hearing how my people felt, it made me think later, 'What if I had stayed silent?'"

The Exponential Effect

13

Organizations are living systems in which people are connecting all the time. In fact, you can picture each TouchPoint as a synapse in your organization's central nervous system, the small distance across which an impulse must pass in order for the next person to engage. Positive impulses stimulate change; negative ones block it. Thus, creating networks where people are poised for change requires transmitting positive impulses, frequently and consistently. When you are fully aware of the exponential power of TouchPoints, you will see every conversation as a chance to give people a reality check, inspire a sense of the possibilities, or stimulate the desire to change.

TOUGH-MINDED ON THE ISSUE, TENDER-HEARTED WITH PEOPLE

Times are tough. Whether you are the director of a health clinic, the superintendent of a school, or an entrepreneur creating business software solutions, you must be tough-minded to prevail. Difficult situations pop up every day, performance problems need to be dealt with, and thorny issues need to be addressed in the here and now. In this sense, the global workplace is very Darwinian. You either adapt and prevail, or you die under the weight of mediocre performance. In reality, there is no in-between.

Being tough-minded, however, is no excuse for being brutal. You can be tough on the issues and still be caring with people. In fact, as Doug discovered when he set out to turn Campbell around, you need to build strong relationships and help the people around you grow if you want to achieve sustainable results.

When Doug began his tenure at Campbell, the place was in a funk. Tall fences topped with barbed wire circled buildings that were equally depressing. The carpets were worn, the walls were faded, and the people looked as tired as their surroundings. They had been through a decade of aggressive pricing followed by bone-deep cost cutting, and the company was in a severe downward spiral. Given that reality, Doug began with the premise that for the company to win in the marketplace, it would first need to win in the workplace. That is, Campbell would first need to win the hearts and minds of twenty thousand employees.

Show That You Care

On Doug's first day at work, a company-wide meeting was held to introduce him as the new CEO. At that meeting, he made a promise to all the employees that ultimately became known as **The Campbell Promise**: *Campbell Valuing People, People Valuing Campbell*. His point was that the leaders must show that they cared about the employees' agenda before they could expect the employees to care about the company's agenda. To show that he meant what he said, Doug began to look for ways to tangibly demonstrate that he cared, by asking everyone he ran into, "What can we do better?" "How can I help?"

One day Pat, the head of the global supply chain, answered, "This place looks like a high-security prison. How about we get rid of those rusty fences and all that barbed wire?" Doug replied, "Let's do it!"

To follow up and show his support, Doug dropped by Pat's office regularly, asking, "Where are you on the plans for more security?" "Have you picked a contractor for the new fencing?" "Can we put a fresh coat of paint on the curbs?" "How about sprucing up the landscaping as well?" Those kinds of small interactions are the best-kept secret of leadership. They are the TouchPoints that take an idea and make it real.

Within a few months, there was clear evidence that someone cared: improved security, discreet fences, and bright yellow curbs. On a roll, the maintenance group then tackled the building interiors by painting the hallways, putting in new carpeting, and hanging up new pictures. Over time, other people began to come up with ideas that went beyond the physical environment: What about starting affinity networks? What about experimenting with more flexible hours? Before long, the exponential effect was spreading throughout the company, infusing everyone with a revived sense of the possibilities: What about better-for-you soups, more convenient packaging, stronger brand messages...?

The Campbell Promise was compelling because it was heartfelt and relevant to the situation, and also because it spoke to people in a language they understood. The leaders showed they genuinely cared about the people, and the people came out fighting for the company. A promise had been made and kept.

Set High Standards

While Doug was seeking to inspire trust, he also established tougher and measurable leadership standards. This led Campbell to use the Gallup metric to track the level of employee engagement.[1] In this case, the gold standard was an engagement ratio of 12:1, meaning that, broadly speaking, each leader would need to have twelve employees who were enthusiastic about their work for every one who was disenchanted.

In 2001, Doug got the baseline results from the Gallup survey. He knew things would be bad, but even he had not anticipated an engagement ratio that was less than 2:1. It didn't help when the Gallup engagement manager said,

---

[1]The Gallup employee engagement database includes more than thirty years of in-depth behavioral economic research involving more than seventeen million employees. Gallup's latest meta-analysis (an analysis of data from more than 152 organizations) shows dramatic differences between top- and bottom-quartile workgroups on key business outcomes. Beyond the significant differences engaged workgroups show in productivity, profitability, safety incidents, and absenteeism versus disengaged workgroups, the research also proves that engaged organizations' earnings per share growth rate is 3.9 times greater than that of organizations with lower engagement in their same industry. For more information, see Gallup, "Employee Engagement: A Leading Indicator for Financial Performance," www.gallup.com/consulting/52/employee-engagement.aspx.

"These are the worst results I have ever seen for a Fortune 500 firm!"

To raise the engagement level, Doug needed all of the 350 global-level leaders to do their part, because they were the ones who touched every department and corner of the company. But after two years of training, coaching, and cajoling, the engagement level had barely moved. It was clear that too many leaders were only modestly on board, and a modest commitment was simply not good enough.

Doug began the 2003 global leadership meeting by putting up the latest engagement level scores—a 4:1 engagement ratio. Then he looked at the group and said quietly but in a forceful tone, "Enough is enough." He told them that his expectations were *not* changing; in fact, they were becoming more demanding. "I hope all of you want to be part of this company going forward, but you have to lead in a way that's going to build the world's most extraordinary food company. If you don't want to sign up for that, you shouldn't be here." The room became very quiet. People were stunned. Doug was always so composed, but at that moment there was no doubt he had had it. People still reminisce about that TouchPoint: "That was the day Doug got up his Irish." "It was great to really see the man's convictions." "Doug was pretty strong, but it was time."

By the end of that year and less than three years into his tenure, nearly 300 of the 350 global leaders had left or had been asked to leave the organization. These were gritty and trying times for Doug and everyone involved, which required a massive number of very difficult conversations and encounters virtually every week. Leaders had to make tough decisions, people had to be let go, organizations had to be reengineered, and employees had to be reassured. No one was immune.

On the positive side, the leaders who were let go were replaced by a new breed of leaders who were highly competent, knew how to tap into people's potential, and were very performance oriented. Soon things began to change. In 2006, the Gallup ratio was 6:1; in 2007 it was 9:1; in 2008, the 12:1 gold standard was reached; and by 2010, the engagement ratio was an astonishing 17:1!

WHAT'S YOUR APPROACH?

No leader can succeed by being only tough-minded or only tender-hearted. Every day there will be TouchPoints in which you need to focus on results and others in which you deal with relationships, moments when you must push to make a deadline and others when you need to stop everything and listen. Every day, you need to be both tough-minded on the issue *and* tender-hearted with people.

Of course, some leaders tend to be bold and direct and others more considerate. Some are more adept at confronting the facts and others at tuning in to the feelings. Which approach feels more comfortable to you?

The Tough-Minded Approach

Many leaders love to take on issues related to performance. They enjoy focusing on goals, setting the
standards, creating a sense of urgency, sticking to the task,
and competing to win. If that is your strength, you
probably like to keep things simple. When faced with bad
news, you tackle it head-on. When people fall short, you
tell them directly. When there is a conflict, you deal with
it. You move quickly and act decisively.

But you need to be careful, because any strength taken
to an extreme can become a liability. When that happens,
the people on your team may hold on to the ball when
they should be passing it. They may ignore problems that
do not affect their own personal targets and rewards. As
a leader, you may even cross the line between not tolerating poor performance (which results in high standards)
and not tolerating mistakes (which leads to compliance).

Leaders who prefer the tough-minded approach
sometimes get twitchy when we talk about being tender-
hearted. To them it sounds too touchy-feely, and they get
visions of sitting in circles and singing "Kumbaya." But
being tender-hearted is not about group hugs or invading
other people's privacy. It simply means that you see each
employee as a human being and therefore worthy of
respect.

The Tender-Hearted Approach

For other leaders, the people come first. Such leaders like to set the direction, provide a few guidelines, leverage people's talents and passion, and get out of the way. They like to build high-trust partnerships and push for win-win solutions. If that is your strength, then you are good at listening, you involve others, and you focus on people's potential. You expect the members of your team to look out for one another, and you make it clear that anyone's failure is everyone's failure.

But just as being tough-minded can become a liability when it is taken to extremes, there is a dark side to the tender-hearted approach. For example, the team may become wonderfully inventive at passing the ball, but no one drives for the goal. People may value consensus more than progress or get bent out of shape over little things. In addition, you may forget that it is more important for a leader to be trusted (which sometimes involves making tough calls) than to be liked.

■ ■

As you reflect on these two approaches, where are you strong? When things get tense, what is your default setting? Where could you do better?

If you are out of balance, the solution is not to lower the volume where you are strong but to dial up in the area where you are less comfortable or feel less capable. For example, if you are intensely competitive, you must also be able to show compassion when someone is going through a difficult time. If people usually come first with you, you must still be prepared to step in—forcefully at times—when someone violates a principle. In either case, you want to act in a way that is genuine and that leads to stronger results and relationships. When you are strong at doing both, you can be amazingly effective.

In addition to reflecting on your own approach, think about the people you work with. What is their dominant style? If you and your colleagues approach a TouchPoint in meaningfully different ways, you might have to work harder at making a positive connection.

For example, Lisa, a VP who led an innovation team of eighteen people, was struggling in her attempts to influence some of her peers. She was especially concerned about her relationship with one colleague whose support was critical to the success of a new initiative. Finally, she asked him to meet with her privately and did something she had never done before: she let down her guard. She talked about her values and explained why she cared so much about her work. Then she said, "I want us to have a strong working relationship. Can you tell me what you look for in a colleague? What does it take for you to trust someone?"

It turned out that whereas Lisa valued being tough on results, her colleague really cared about relationships. She thought it was admirable to take the issues head-on; he trusted people who were loyal and open to other people's points of view. These were powerful insights for both of them, and this TouchPoint became a turning point in the way they worked together.

Be Tough-Minded *and* Tender-Hearted

When you are both tough-minded and tender-hearted, you can deliver ever-higher levels of performance. One summer evening, Mette received a phone call from Jens Moberg, a former client. He had just finished his first year as corporate VP at Microsoft, responsible for customer service and sales, and his team had aced it! He was excited about the year ahead: "Mette, here is my idea: I want to make $7 billion in 2007 by building high-trust teams."

That one-sentence statement was vintage Jens, because it captured his intense commitment to both the results and the relationships. To Jens, the secret to hitting the $7 billion mark was to get out and work directly with each of the fourteen regions and to design a way to stay in touch throughout the year. Over the next year, Jens invested about twenty days of his own time helping people move from thinking "me" to thinking "we," and it paid off. By the end of the year, trust was up, the top performers were collaborating, and the teams beat the company's forecast.

THE POINT IS . . .

In this fast-moving, intensely complex, global workplace, many things are beyond your control. Fortunately, there are two things that are entirely within your control. The first is that you can choose to bring a sense of positive energy and direction to your very next TouchPoint, and then do it again. The second is that you can choose to stretch yourself as a leader and aim for mastery (more about that in the next chapter).

To get started right away, simply take the next unplanned interaction as an opportunity to help. Maybe you can ask the right question to help someone get a little clearer, or maybe you can reinforce the importance of a project to help a team become a little more committed.

Now think about what might happen if you were to be helpful to others three times a day for the next week. How would that feel? What if you were to do it again next week, and the week after that? Twenty TouchPoints a week in which you made a difference would add up to more than a thousand such TouchPoints in a year. This would be a very small commitment, yet the impact would be significant, because you would not only feel more in control of your time but also gain more influence.

The beauty of TouchPoint leadership is that it is both approachable and aspirational. Although it is easy to do well in two or three TouchPoints each day, doing it a dozen times a day, and doing it consistently day after day, is an entirely different matter. The pursuit of mastery is a lifelong journey, and that journey begins on the very next page.

2
The Commitment to Mastery

THE CHOICE IS YOURS

Leaders are doers. They build things, grow things, and move things forward. They shape the future by doing something better or bolder or more exciting. Unlike many who only dream of creating a better future, leaders are the dreamers who get things done, and the way they do that is by influencing others. First-line leaders create the energy and direction to lift the performance of their teams. Leaders of leaders do it by engaging an entire department, division, or organization.

The greater your responsibility, the larger the number of variables and the more skilled you need to be. The higher up you go, the greater the number of people who are watching you, and the more consistent you must be. Furthermore, each time you are promoted, your new peers are likely to have more experience and stronger ideas about how to lead. To influence them, your voice must be so clear that they can hear you and so credible that they will pay attention to you. To gain such a level of credibility, it is not enough merely to *use* TouchPoints—you need to *master* them.

All too often, experts or top performers seek leadership positions because those positions are the only way to get more pay, perks, prestige, or power. Once they are in the role, however, many discover they don't like the increased visibility, responsibility, and pressure.

Consider for a moment how intense the work is for a coach of a major league basketball or football team. Yet such coaches may deal with fewer than a hundred athletes and support personnel, whereas a leader of leaders may have hundreds, if not thousands, of "players" on the field at one time. In addition, these players are often part of virtual teams, spread across multiple time zones. Even if all of a leader's team members are in one location, he or she may be dealing with union and nonunion employees, maintenance people and truck drivers, engineers and marketers, and so forth. The complexity is enormous.

To succeed in the work of leadership, you need to be good at it. And to become really good at it, you have to prepare. Frankly, if you don't love the pressure, the sweat, and the grind, it just isn't worth it. Life is too short to be halfhearted about your work. More important, people deserve someone worth following.

That is the reason we encourage you to make the commitment to mastery.

BARRIERS TO MASTERY

The closer you get to mastery, the better able you are to take everyday moments and infuse them with something *extra*. That extra may be a thumbs-up or a pat on the back. It may be hearing someone out or taking the time to explain why something matters. That extra is what transforms ordinary interactions into *extra*ordinary ones. Astute leaders invest in these TouchPoints because they know that the net sum of the connections determines the health of the relationships, and the vitality of the relationships equals the strength of the unit. The payoff is a cohesive team that can move quickly and effectively.

Given these advantages, why doesn't everyone seek mastery? In our experience, there are three common reasons, and one of them may apply to you.

You are too stressed. You are getting pinged, dinged, zapped, inundated, and overwhelmed. You have twenty balls in the air, and just as you manage to juggle those, someone tosses you two more. It seems like you are always behind. If you are doing well at work, you are falling short at home. If you are making more time for your family, you feel you are letting down your team. The last thing you need is one more area where you are not measuring up.

Clearly such a situation is not sustainable. Although you might develop a reputation for being a hard worker, you certainly will not be seen as a candidate for greater responsibilities or more complex challenges. Don't wait until you slip and fall off the treadmill. Step off now!

You are quite comfortable. Maybe you have been in your job for a number of years. You are good at what you do, and you are respected. You may have a boss who is not too hot or too cold, a job that is not too big or too small, and expectations that are not too hard or too soft. That's great—except that when people get too comfortable, they often become less vigilant. They stop foraging for new learning and lose their edge.

Consider this piece of data: research has found that the brains of domesticated animals are 15 to 30 percent smaller than those of their wild counterparts.[1] So if you want to thrive in a fiercely competitive global environment, you need to stay a little wild. You need to be alert and continuously update your skills. Today's organizations draw on the best talent from all over the world. This means that the standards keep going up, and you need to get better just to stay in place.

You are new to your role. When you take on new responsibilities, you tend to focus on understanding all the technical dimensions of the role. You think that you simply don't have time to aim for mastery. Yet these are

[1]John Medina, *Brain Rules* (Seattle: Pear Press, 2008), p. 58.

precisely the times when you need to stretch yourself, because as a leader, you are totally dependent on other people to do a good job. These are the times when you must make connections so quickly that people will be forthcoming about the current reality. These are the times when you must speak so clearly that everyone gets the same message. These are the times when you need to listen so intently that everyone feels heard. When you choose to develop both your technical and TouchPoint capabilities, you will accelerate your learning and lift your performance.

MAKE TIME FOR MASTERY

At this point, you might be thinking, "This all makes sense, but I still don't have the time!" Guess what: those who are committed to mastery also don't have the time; they make the time. As with anything you value in life—being a good parent or a good friend, getting an advanced degree, or running a marathon—you simply need to make mastery a priority.

"Getting clear about what is important has changed my whole game," says Mike, president of a large national sales force. Mike's days were jam-packed with issues and people, the pressure was intense, and Mike was known to get testy at times.

"Now I block out time at the beginning and the end of each day," he continued, "and my people know not to mess with my calendar before nine and after four." This is Mike's time to think, to strategize, and to visualize how he wants to handle the tough meetings. Securing this mental space allows him to be completely present when he engages with other people. "The rest of the time, I am 100 percent available and can easily address six issues in an hour."

The results have been gratifying. "Today I explode about half as often, and when I do it's only half as bad. People are really noticing. They think I'm happier. Calmer. One even asked if I was doing yoga." Even Mike's wife says he is less tired and grumpy when he gets home.

When you choose to make mastering the TouchPoint a priority, here is a tip for how to find some time. Take a look at your calendar and estimate how many of your meetings *you* initiate. Mike was amazed to discover that he was the one who set up most of the early-morning conference calls and more than half of his other meetings.

No matter what the number is for you, we encourage you to schedule only half as many meetings next week, or to schedule the same number but make them half as long. That way you can build some thinking time into your day and make room for unforeseen TouchPoints. But that also means that when a TouchPoint begins—*be there!* Focus on the issue, look for ways to be helpful, and do everything you can to advance the agenda.

Another reason people are reluctant to go for mastery is that it can seem overwhelming. In fact, even the word *mastery* can seem daunting. But just as a journey of a thousand miles begins with a single step, so the road to mastery begins by simply asking yourself the question, *What's one thing I could do better tomorrow?* Just one thing! Then each day you become a little better than the day before, each week you become quite a bit better than the previous week, and each quarter you become noticeably better.

THE MASTERY ESSENTIALS

If you aspire to mastery, you must use your head, use your heart, and use your hands. That is, you need a *logical* model that guides your approach to leading people and change (head), a clear sense of purpose and an *authentic* way of engaging with others (heart), and practices that enable you to be prepared and *competent* in the moment (hands).

These three essentials are not a prescription for the "right" way to lead. They are simply a structured approach to developing *your* way of mobilizing and organizing people, *your* brand as a leader, *your* unique touch.

Your touch is where the three strands (head, heart, and hands) come together in the art of the moment, enabling you to make clear judgments in the TouchPoint. When you have the touch, you can have a dozen balls in the air and juggle them with apparent ease. You may stand in the midst of escalating tensions and naturally diffuse them. You can make split-second decisions in a way that seems effortless to others. The way you do all that is by blocking out the noise, stripping away everything extraneous, and being fully present to the possibilities of the moment.

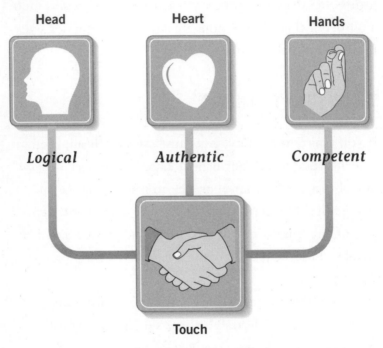

The Mastery Essentials

Use Your Head

To begin with, you need a clear approach to leadership. As a leader, you must be prepared to parse through countless data points, detect the patterns, and frame what is going on in the TouchPoint. To do so quickly, intelligently, and consistently, you need to create a personal leadership model that works for you in your unique situation.

Ward Clapham, chief of the Richmond detachment of the Royal Canadian Mounted Police (RCMP), is absolutely clear about his model, which is centered around "prepare and repair." This model guides everything he does, including the way he deals with at-risk teens, handles criminals, engages with community leaders, and develops his officers.

Instead of waiting until something goes wrong and then moving to fix it, Ward does everything he can to get ahead of the problem. This approach is evident throughout the detachment. For example, consider a typical police department's *internal investigation unit*, which waits until an officer does something wrong before intervening. Ward got ahead of the problem by renaming it the *internal prevention unit* and expanding its responsibilities to include implementing standards as well as conducting investigations. By being accountable for preventing problems, in just one year the unit accomplished a 70 percent reduction in complaints against police officers.

As a leader, Ward is so clear that he passes the exponential test. All the Mounties in his unit not only understand his model; they even tell their peers in other detachments about it.

What if you had an equally clear way of thinking about how to lead your team or department? How would that increase your level of influence?

Use Your Heart

Next, you need to become incredibly clear about your intentions so that you can develop a healthy and dynamic core. Think about the core of a golfer, the axis around which the rest of the body rotates when he takes a swing. Having a strong core allows him to wind up the body's inherent energy and release it in a natural and controlled way—contact!—until the rotation is completed. To achieve such grace and power in the moment, you need to be very clear about who you are and why you choose to lead. You need to have the heart for leadership.

Take Irene, president of a $1 billion business unit. Among the people who have had a powerful influence on her as a leader, she names her mother and grandmother, two women who taught her about resilience. Whatever she comes up against is nothing, Irene says, compared to what they went through as they fled Shanghai and faced near-starvation during the Second World War.

Irene is irrepressible when it comes to turning around poorly performing business units. She gives 100 percent to the job, and she expects the same from the people around her. Passionate about what she does, she has no patience with the "What's in it for me?" attitude. In her view, "If you can't put the organization's interest ahead of your own comfort and change your behaviors, then you have no business being here." Irene attracts some of the best talent because, although she expects a lot, she gives even more. As she says, "It's all about working together, building those eyeball-to-eyeball, prick-your-finger-and-share-blood relationships."

Consider the relationships on your team. What might you achieve if everyone on your team put the group's goals before his or her individual interests?

Use Your Hands

Finally, you need to become clearly competent so that you can engage with confidence and extend that confidence to others in every interaction. You need to be able to draw on a variety of skills so that regardless of what is thrown at you, you can handle it. You may need to diffuse tension with humor, push people by asking tough questions, or tell stories that stick. Whatever is needed, you want to do it skillfully.

One powerful practice is to lead with listening. Consider Bergit (not her real name), a team leader with Microsoft in Norway. In a 360-degree feedback session, Bergit got slammed for her behavior during one-on-one meetings with her direct reports. They were annoyed by the way her eyes kept darting to scan incoming messages while they were talking.

When Bergit realized that her lack of attention made people feel that she didn't care, she changed her behavior—and that changed everything. From then on, when it was time for a weekly one-on-one session, she and her team member would put on their boots and coats (they were in Norway, after all) and go for a walk, leaving their PDAs behind. As a result, not only was Bergit able to devote her full attention to helping the other person, but the two of them brought a fresh, natural, high-energy feeling back to the office.

What if your team asked you to adopt a new behavior that, in their eyes, would make you a better leader—and you did it? What if you did it again, and again? In addition to becoming better yourself, you would also earn their respect and the right to ask them to make changes to their behavior.

■ ■

If you like the *idea* of mastery but wonder whether it is worth the price, take a moment to consider the costs of not aiming for mastery.

MISSING THE MARK

For all of us, there are days when we don't have our head in the game; there are times when our heart isn't in it; and there are situations where we simply haven't had the time to prepare. That said, we all tend to have one essential on which we trip up so often that it keeps us from moving toward mastery.

No Underlying Logic

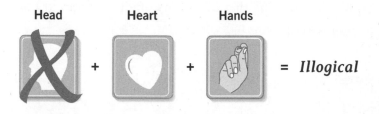

When you don't have a clear approach to leadership, people don't understand *why* you make the calls you do. *Why* was that project given to another department? *Why* don't they get that report anymore? *Why* were the targets adjusted again? People search for the underlying logic, but it doesn't seem to be there. They may see you begin every quarter talking about farming and growing a strong relationship with customers, but by the end of the quarter, you are back to using hunting and eat-what-you-kill metaphors. Instead of people saying, "That makes sense," "What a great way of framing it," or "So that's why it's so important," they leave meetings commiserating: "I just don't get it," "Why exactly did we have to do this?" or "I'm confused." Then they pass that confusion on to others, creating an exponentially muddled effect.

Why does this happen? It may be because you have many great ideas but haven't yet developed the mental discipline to set priorities. Perhaps the complexities of your new position are enormous, and you haven't yet built the mental muscle to figure things out, or you need to respond to conditions that keep changing. It could be that your thinking is very clear, but you don't take the time to explain it, believing that the others ought to figure it out by themselves.

No Genuine Connection

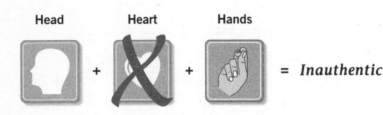

When you don't know (or don't show) what's in your heart, you cannot make a real connection with others. You may genuinely care about the people on your team, but if they can't tell your true feelings, why should they trust you? Also, if you don't convey what you care about, they are less likely to be forthcoming with their own cares and concerns. After all, why should they risk themselves in this relationship if you don't? Consequently, instead of lighting up the synapses with enthusiasm, you are left with tepid connections and commitments. Your team members, rather than telling their colleagues, "I'm so excited to be part of her team," "I don't want to let him down," or

"I know she has my back," say things like "I just can't read him," "He pretends that he wants our input, but he really doesn't," or "I don't know when she last said 'thank you.'"

If you don't have the heart for leadership, don't do it. If you *do* love the work but don't know how to show it, figure out what's holding you back. Maybe you feel awkward talking about your passion and purpose, seeing them as something private. Such sensibilities are fine for an individual contributor, but things change when you become a leader. When you gain positional authority, you also gain the power to promote or demote people, so their future is partly in your hands. Thus they are constantly on the alert for signals, trying to figure out what matters most to you.

No Solid Skills

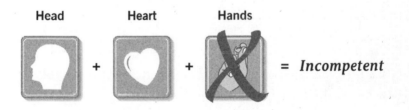

Head + **Heart** + **Hands** = *Incompetent*

When you don't do your homework, people can't count on you to prepare and put forth your best effort. They just don't feel as though they're in good hands with you as a leader. Furthermore, when you don't make honing your skills a priority, why should they bother? Thus your own lack of discipline not only undermines *your* credibility but also may affect your department's reputation. You might say it can lead to exponential ineptitude. Instead of people saying, "It's a pleasure to watch her in action," "He's always prepared," or "He is such a pro," they mutter, "He's too impulsive," "She was in over her head on that one," or "It's hit or miss with him; he's just not consistent."

Maybe you don't practice because you are used to being the smartest kid on the block and able to wing it. Maybe you confuse working hard with working out, thinking that by putting in long hours you automatically get better. As the responsibilities and the complexities increase, however, winging it is no longer good enough, and working more hours is no longer an option. Something has to change.

■ ■

We all fall short in some areas—even the masters mess up. As you consider the three essentials, you may realize that you need to explain things better or need to be more forthcoming. Or it could be that you just need to stop talking so much and listen more. No one expects you to be perfect, but they do look for you to improve.

But making such changes is hard. That is because you need to work at it until your new insight drops from your head to your hands, so that you don't have to think much about it. You need to practice until your best intentions drop from your heart to your hands and become almost instinctive. That is what Bill, a VP of manufacturing, did this past year.

Bill explains, "When I started as a leader, my attitude was 'Damn the torpedoes.' 'If we are not number 1, why are we there?' I was really impatient, and I would constantly finish people's sentences."

Then Bill got some tough 360-degree feedback. "It was there in black and white staring me in my face, and I knew I had to change." He did just one thing differently. "I stopped talking. When people came up to me, I'd really listen. Then, when they seemed done, I'd give them a chance to add something by asking, 'Is there something else?' It was simply a matter of having the discipline to do that." Today Bill sees listening as his way to show people he truly cares about what they say.

The change has been so dramatic that his team talks about "the new Bill" and "the old Bill," joking about what the old Bill would have said in a particular TouchPoint.

CHECK HOW YOU ARE DOING

Just as a master builder can check the quality of his work by dropping a plumb line, so you can use the three Touch-Point essentials to check your progress toward mastery. A quick glance at the "checklist" illustrated here can tell you where you are hitting the mark and where you are missing it.

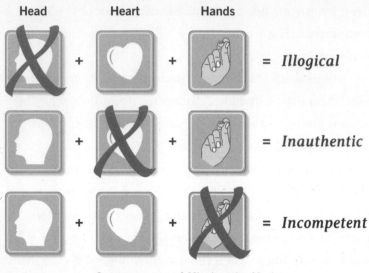

Consequences of Missing the Mark

Mary, a VP of human resources serving forty-five hundred employees in the Asia Pacific region, finds that checking the essentials is useful even when it comes to her leaders' career development. "Thinking 'head,' 'heart,' and 'hands' is such a quick way to discern a leader's strengths, and, conversely, his or her area of vulnerability. I use it all the time. Most leaders have outages, and this helps me figure out how I can help."

MAKE A PROMISE TO YOURSELF

Making a promise to yourself is easy; the hard part is keeping it.

Imagine the following scenario. Someone calls you with an urgent request to meet. You agree. You arrive at the appointed time, but the person doesn't show up, and after a while you leave. A few hours later, the person calls again, apologizes profusely, and pleads with you to meet. Once again, you agree. Once again, the person is a no-show. Then, almost unbelievably, the same thing happens a third time.

How would you describe such a person? Words like "flaky," "untrustworthy," and "unreliable" undoubtedly come to mind.

But wait! Have you ever made an appointment with yourself and then not shown up? Have you ever said, "On Monday morning, I will begin my diet," "After this deadline is over, I'll make more time for my family," or "When I settle into my new position, then I'll make time to improve my leadership"? Only, at the appointed time, you don't show up.

The reason that happens is that in the space between our best intentions and our actions lies something vital: the depth of our commitment. And the greater the task, the more intense that commitment needs to be.

The secret to making a strong commitment is to want something badly enough. Remember what it was like when, as a child, you really, really wanted something? Remember how incredibly persistent you could be? You would do anything from washing the dishes to mowing the lawn. And you would cajole and pester your parents until they gave in. When it comes to leadership, what do you want with that same level of intensity?

Maybe your ambition is to be in the top 1 percent in your organization, so that you will have a shot at the top job. Maybe you need to recover from a spectacular setback. Maybe your dream is for the team to achieve a near-impossible target. Or perhaps your family is your top priority right now, and what you want most of all is to become so efficient that you can get your work done faster and go home earlier.

THE POINT IS . . .

The average leader doesn't change until the cost of *not* changing becomes greater than the cost of changing. That may happen when he gets a bad performance review, something blows up in his face, or he lands in a job where he feels that he's in over his head.

Leaders who want to be influential, in contrast, look at leadership as something they must get really good at. Because they work at it, they improve, which makes them feel more committed, so they practice more and continue to accelerate their own development.

Several years ago, at the beginning of a one-week executive retreat at Sundance, Utah, Mette asked one of the participants, "Why are you here?" He dropped his head toward his left shoulder and said, "Because my brain is like this!" (meaning he was extremely left-brained and highly analytical). Then he grabbed the hair on top of his head, pulled his head back up to midline, and continued, "I have been told that if I can't get my head up here, I've had my last promotion." That had gotten his attention! People were telling him that he was all head and hands, and although that had been adequate to get him to where he was now, he would need more than technical competencies to move to the next level.

Although receiving such feedback hurts, it is often one of the best things that happen to you as a leader. The reason is that humility softens the ground for new learning and real growth. (It's no coincidence that the word *humility* comes from the Latin *humus*, meaning "ground.")

In fact, the people who are the most committed to mastering their craft are often the most humble. That is because, instead of comparing themselves to others, they are moved by an inner vision of what they might achieve.

Peter F. Drucker, the quintessential management thinker, shares a story of such a master in his article "My Life as a Knowledge Worker." When Drucker was barely eighteen years old and living in Hamburg, he went to see the Verdi opera *Falstaff*. Drucker was astonished by the opera's incredible vitality and Verdi's zest for life, and even more so when he learned that Verdi had been eighty years old when he composed it. Why would Verdi, already one of the greatest composers of his time, write this exceedingly demanding work at such an advanced age? Drucker found the answer in Verdi's own words: "All my life as a musician, I have striven for perfection. It has always eluded me. I surely had an obligation to make one more try."[2]

The question is, what type of leader do you want to be? Do you want to be the leader who waits around for the make-or-break moment, or do you want to be the one who gets in front of it? Whatever your aspiration, do you want it enough to make the commitment to mastery?

[2]Peter Drucker, "My Life as a Knowledge Worker," *Inc.*, February 1997, pp. 76–78.

3

Use Your Head

THE COMMITMENT
TO INQUIRY

At the age of twenty-three, Roger was hired by
Unilever to oversee a hundred people on the packing
floor of a factory in North London. Three weeks after he
started, the company announced that the site would be
closed down the following year.

A few months later, a woman came up and told Roger
that she just realized that she had inadvertently "packed
her apple" sometime during the last ninety minutes. Roger
was faced with a problem: he had a rogue apple somewhere, encased in a 200g pot of face cream, boxed in a
carton, wrapped on a tray, packed in a box, and loaded on
a pallet, heading for the export market. What to do?

Roger decided to recall the pallets. He and the team
spent the next two hours searching for the "damn apple."
After it was found, the whole thing seemed so silly that

everyone burst out laughing, and the infamous apple became part of plant folklore during its last months of operations.

Why did Roger make that call? He could have let the apple go through. In fact, before this shipment could get into the hands of a customer halfway around the world, the plant would already be shut down. But to Roger's way of thinking about leadership, maintaining people's respect was paramount. His assumption was that if he didn't hold the line on this seemingly small issue, he would lose credibility, which would make leading them through the plant closure even more difficult than it would otherwise be.

Like Roger, we each have our own ideas about what works. They may be things we have picked up along the way, favorite bits of advice, stock phrases, and maxims to live by. Using your head is about taking this patchwork of ideas and assumptions and transforming them into a coherent set of ideas. We refer to this set of ideas as your personal *leadership model.*

Developing a leadership model is one of the most practical, energy-saving, and stress-reducing things you can do as a leader. That is because the clearer *your* thinking becomes in the TouchPoint, the less *the others* will waste their time wondering about how you might approach an issue or make a call. Instead, they will be able to anticipate your decisions and act with confidence, often without having to consult with you. This gives *them* more autonomy and *you* more thinking time.

To lead effectively in a TouchPoint, you need a model that is uniquely relevant to your situation, one that can engage people and improve performance. Every leader's model is different, because everyone's situation is different. Thus our aim is not to convert you to our ways of seeing things but to encourage you to find your own answers. You don't need to discover and illuminate universal Truths, with a capital *T*. You just need to find an increasingly useful explanation for how your world works.

MODELS GUIDE OUR BEHAVIOR

We use models all the time to think through a problem and figure out what to do about it. The secret to an effective model is to base it on an ever-better understanding of the nature of things. For example, if you have ever tried to lose weight, the first thing you do is decide on a mental model for how to go about it. You may go on a high-protein or low-fat diet or cut down your intake of carbohydrates; eat as usual but exercise harder; eat only the calories you need to survive; or use a combination of different approaches.

Although each model relies on the same understanding of human physiology that says you will lose weight if you use up more calories than you consume, the outcomes will differ. You may shed pounds quickly or gradually, achieve short-term or sustainable results, become lethargic or energized. To lose the weight and keep it off, you need to develop your own unique model, one that will work for you given your goals, lifestyle, body type, health, and more.

Likewise, when it comes to leadership, you need a mental model that is based on a good understanding of human nature and the nature of change. Again, there are many possible approaches: you can make all the decisions and tell people what to do, or you can help them make decisions and take action on their own; you can instill a sense of competition or a sense of collaboration; you can create an environment that punishes people for mistakes or one that rewards them for taking risks. Each approach relies on its own line of logic and will have different outcomes. Just as someone else's diet plan is not likely to fit you perfectly, someone else's leadership model is unlikely to be a perfect fit for your situation.

When you have a meaningful model, you can be immensely helpful during even the briefest TouchPoint. That is because your model will help you sort through all the facts and feelings, frame the issue in a way that makes sense, and make good judgment calls. Also, by having a robust model you will become consistent from TouchPoint to TouchPoint, so the others will experience an underlying logic, making it easier for them to understand your decisions and explain them to others.

MODELS, MODELS, EVERYWHERE

At this stage in your career, you are likely to have been inundated with models and frameworks, and you can always count on the latest business book or *Harvard Business Review* article to champion yet another approach to leadership. You might be thinking, "Given the many good ideas out there, why not just adopt one of those?"

One reason is that when you stand in the heat of the moment, faced with serious delays or inexcusable errors, your first thought won't be, "What would management expert Ken Blanchard do?" Instead, you will default to your own way of thinking about leadership.

The other answer is that, in the words of George E. P. Box, a pioneer in quality control, "All models are wrong but some are useful."[1] Even Doug, a terminal student of leadership, has never found just the right model for him. That is because all those models and theories have been crafted independently from who he is and from his unique set of circumstances. Think about it: it would be amazingly serendipitous if a model that was crafted separately from your situation would be an *exact* fit for how you ought to lead.

That being said, Box also makes the point that the generic models are useful. That is why you want to steep

[1] George E. P. Box, "Robustness in the Strategy of Scientific Model Building," in R. L. Launer and G. N. Wilkinson, eds., *Robustness in Statistics: Proceedings of a Workshop* (New York: Academic Press, 1979), p. 40.

yourself in the classics and keep up on the latest research and innovations. Then consider the ideas that look most promising and use them as inspiration for your own leadership model.

That is what Doug did when he crafted the Campbell Leadership Model.

THE CAMPBELL LEADERSHIP MODEL

To come up with a leadership model that would be right for Campbell, Doug borrowed concepts from the classics (the work of Warren Bennis, Stephen Covey, Jim Collins, Meg Wheatley, John Kotter, and others) that he had resonated with over the years and found to be useful. Then he thought about his many years of experience and what had enabled him to lead a number of very difficult turnarounds. Along the way, he jotted down ideas and discussed them with members of his team.

When he was ready, he and a team of executives crafted the Campbell Leadership Model. It is a six-part circular model in which the first action is to *Inspire Trust* and the last action is to *Produce Extraordinary Results*—which, in turn, increases credibility and inspires more trust, creating a self-reinforcing loop. The model emphasizes high-trust behaviors, because Doug believed that Campbell's leaders would need to gain the trust of the employees before they could expect the employees to volunteer their best ideas and energy.

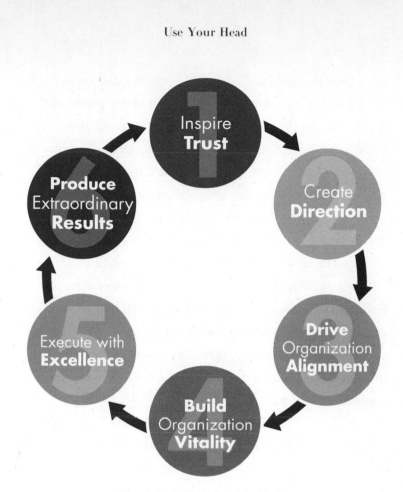

The Campbell Leadership Model

Once the model had been crafted and tested, it became an integral part of how the leaders in the company think and behave in a TouchPoint. By listening carefully, they can quickly assess the issue and determine whether the problem is one of trust, direction, alignment, and so forth. Because they share a common language, they can then zero in on the area of concern and together find the best solution.

Given the wide use of the Campbell Leadership Model within the company, one could argue that there is no need for the organization's leaders to develop their own. But the model Doug and his team created serves the company as a whole. Other leaders still need to do their own thinking and create a model that speaks to who they are and the unique needs of their departments or divisions. The heads of legal, marketing, and operations start out with their own mental models and face such different realities that they each need to find their own way to effectively approach people and change. Of course, because each area is part of the larger corporate context, the leaders also need to ensure a meaningful overlap between their own models and the company's.

In the CEO Institute, participants create leadership models by first becoming exposed to the best thinking available. After reading several books and articles and attending the World Business Forum, they engage in discussions about the ideas that resonate most with them. Afterwards, they look for their own answers to two vital leadership questions and bring everything together by creating several prototypes of their leadership model. Then they explain their models to one another. It is exciting to see how different these prototypes are, yet they all make good sense.

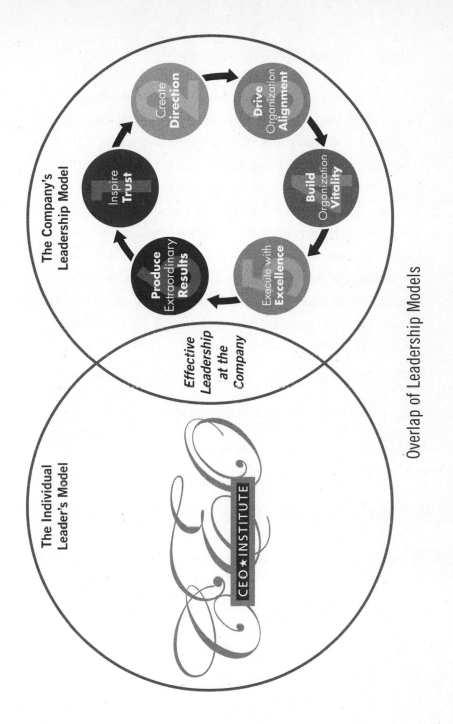

The Company's Leadership Model

Create **Direction**

Drive Organization **Alignment**

Inspire **Trust**

Build Organization **Vitality**

Produce Extraordinary **Results**

Execute with **Excellence**

Effective Leadership at the Company

The Individual Leader's Model

CEO★INSTITUTE

Overlap of Leadership Models

MAKE A COMMITMENT TO INQUIRY

The first step in creating your own leadership model is
to become aware of your current assumptions—the ways
in which you almost instinctively think about people and
performance—so that you can take a clear-eyed look at
how well those assumptions work. Next, you search for
the answers to two vital leadership questions by drawing
inspiration from various sources and thinking about your
own experience. Finally, you organize your answers into
a meaningful flow—an *idea*Pod, if you will, where you
have "downloaded" the best thinking available, added
your own experience, and created a set of ideas that works
for you.

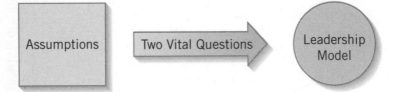

Crafting Your Personal Leadership Model

Of course, your leadership model won't be fixed in
stone. It's an iterative process: you'll apply your model as
issues come up; then you will step outside the situation to
study what is happening as objectively as you can, make
any necessary adjustments, and step back into the thick
of things so that you can test the revised model and see
how it works. That's what it means to have a commitment
to inquiry.

Consider Your Underlying Assumptions

To begin, you first need to surface your assumptions about leadership so that you can assess how effective they are. One way to do that is to think about the metaphors and analogies you gravitate toward. Following are some of the most common ones. As you read them, notice which ones resonate with you.

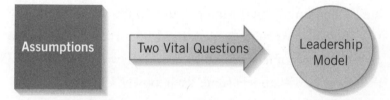

War. For decades, war was the dominant metaphor for leadership. In fact, at one time, Harvard Business School was thought of as the West Point of business, graduating the officer class of corporate America. The professors used expressions such as "rallying the troops," "taking the hill," and "digging strategic moats"; and they made *strategy* and *tactics* ubiquitous business terms. Entrepreneurs, not to be outdone, studied "guerrilla tactics" and learned how to "move swiftly, concentrate their attacks, and win."

Sports. Many leaders use sports analogies when discussing leadership. Depending on whether they want to underline the need for speed or endurance, for brute force or finesse, or for staying the course or adapting, they may compare a difficult challenge to "running a series of sprints" or "back-to-back marathons," or they might tell a story about a basketball team's "come-from-behind victory."

Creativity and community. While Harvard was pushing the competitive approach, Wharton was promoting the advantages of cooperation and creativity. Leaders who are more inclined toward that line of thinking might talk about what it takes to put on a play, do a barn raising, or revitalize a neighborhood, using language such as "creating," "building," "performing," and "pulling together."

Hollywood. As more leaders head up ad hoc teams, many have become attracted to the Hollywood model: the "producer" attracts some "star power" and pulls together the "right players" for a project. Everyone works around the clock until the film is done. When it's "in the can," they are all let go.

Journeys and adventure. Many leaders compare the process of achieving a goal to "taking a journey" (we've done that in this book), using stories about traveling the Silk Road or climbing Mount Everest, with each stage signifying a major milestone, as metaphors for accomplishing something difficult but worthwhile.

Evolution. Other leaders find inspiration in evolution, relating the way that nature uses diversity, experimentation, and redundancies to "adapt and survive" to what an organization can do to succeed. Interestingly, many in today's military also use references from the natural world, as they speak of mobilizing against terrorist "cells" and "simultaneous swarming attacks."

As you read the examples here, which ones fit your way of thinking about leadership most closely? Which resonate the most with you? Then consider the underlying premise of each example. Would you say that the example was built on a belief in

Competition or *collaboration*
Instructing others or *inviting* them
Expanding rapidly or *evolving* gradually
Aiming for *efficiency* or creating *communities*

Most leaders have a bias for one of the words in each pair. Do you? If so, is your bias a strong preference, or do you feel comfortable with both approaches?

At the risk of oversimplifying things, you can think of the word pairs as representing two distinct worldviews, two different ways to think about motivation and change. When you gravitate toward stories that build on the first word in each pair, you will tend toward an *assertive* way of thinking about issues and people. If you are inclined toward stories that build on the second words in the pairs, you will have an *adaptive* approach.

To see how these two mind-sets play out in a Touch-Point, let's consider two scenarios: one about engaging people and the other about leading change.

Engaging people. Let's say you see a frontline employee doing instant messaging instead of making eye contact and greeting every customer. And he keeps doing it! How would you handle this situation?

The *assertive* point of view (based on the assumption that people are rational, economic creatures who look out for their own self-interest) makes this a simple carrot-and-stick task. If that's how you see it, you might reprimand the employee or come up with a new way to entice him to change his behavior. An *adaptive* view (which assumes that human beings are altruistic) might suggest that the employee needs to find meaning in his work. If that's your inclination, you might pull the employee aside to explain what he is expected to do and why it is important.

A third option, however, would be to avoid either of the stereotypical responses. Instead, you might draw on both approaches so that you can get the job done *now* and build capacity for *next time*.

Leading change. Now let us look at how the two stereotypical responses might show up when leading change. Let's say you are in a meeting where the issue is how to deal with incessant delays in the introduction of a new service. In this case, the *assertive* approach would be to dissect the issue, isolate the problem, and come up with a fix, such as replacing equipment or a team leader, providing more training or resources, or changing the metrics. By contrast, the *adaptive* approach would seek to comprehend the system as a whole by looking at the connections and flows of information. The decision in that case might be to strengthen the relationships between two teams, involve the informal leaders, or create a more compelling story about the future.

But why limit yourself to one approach *or* the other? Instead, you could create a solution that involves first fixing an isolated problem and then addressing a deeper and more systemic one.

From our years of study and our experience as a "leader of leaders" and as a "teacher of leaders," here is what has become clear to us: instead of having an *assertive* or *adaptive* approach in the moment, leaders need an *integrated* approach. It makes no sense to think of people as being selfish *or* altruistic, competitive *or* collaborative, because as human beings we are both. Likewise, it is nonsense to look at an organization as if it ought to run like a machine *or* evolve like a living system. Why limit yourself when there are ways to create efficiencies *and* communities? In fact, the best solutions often lie in the creative tension between these natural dualities.

It's interesting to note that the integrative way of thinking has been associated with wisdom for centuries. Ancient Taoist philosophy, for example, sees the assertive *yang* and the adaptive *yin* as the complementary opposites that together form a whole. It is unhealthy to be so caught up in one that you neglect the other. What is healthy is the dynamic integration between the two. Wisdom lies in understanding the movement between the opposites—what Peter Senge (*The Fifth Discipline*) refers to as *the dance of change*.

Answer Two Vital Questions

Your job as a leader is to take people from where they are today to where they need to be tomorrow, do so as quickly as possible, and do it in a way that is sustainable. To accomplish that, you need to master both the "material" and the "process."

Just as a potter must know his material (clay) and understand how to transform it (process) into a strong, functional object, a leader must know her "material" (other people's talent, energy, creativity, and commitment) and understand how to transform that into performance.

To comprehend these basics and how they apply in your culture and context, you need to find your own answers to two vital questions:

1. What makes people give the very best of themselves?
2. What makes for ever-stronger performance in an ever-changing world?

Exploring these questions is a bit like panning for gold: sifting through the clay, dirt, roots, moss, and pebbles to find the real nuggets, the 24-karat insights into human nature and the nature of change. It's a lot of work. So why bother? Because the better you understand the nature of things, the more effective you will become.

Download the Best Thinking

Begin by borrowing from the professors and practition-ers whose research, matrixes, and models have worked for you. Think about the powerful insights you have had over the years, as you watched a movie, read a biography, or listened to a speech. Make a note of these nuggets so that you can use them later.

Think About Your Experience

When it comes to leading others, your experience has already taught you a great deal about what drives people to perform at their best and how you as a leader can create superior performance. Your leadership model should reflect what you have learned from that experience.

As you consider the question *What makes people choose to give the very best of themselves?* think about the way we are all motivated by different things. You might have given your best when you were intent on earning a bonus, seek-ing to gain someone's respect, or excited about solving an intractable problem. But when you think about what drives people, be careful not to assume that just because you are motivated by money, praise, winning, or challenge, others will be as well.

The question is not about what excites *you;* it is about what makes *the other people* engage wholeheartedly. Think about the members of your team. As you bring each person's face to mind, what do you think engages that person—a sense of security, a chance to get ahead, or an opportunity to learn something new? What turns that person off—too much pressure, fear of failure, or not being challenged enough? What about the team as a whole? When are they at their best (that is, passing the ball, cheering each other on, and playing for the team to win)?

As you think about what drives you and others, what are your most critical insights? Were you to guide a high-potential leader, what few nuggets of wisdom could you pass on? What would be your advice to him or her for how to engage people?

Now let's turn to the second question: *What makes for ever stronger performance in an ever changing world?* What are the lessons you have learned about achieving results and then doing it again and again? Have you ever been part of a team that came from behind, beat all the odds, and won? If so, what created the magic? Maybe you joined a team that was already at the top; if you did, what were the key elements that kept it there? Have you ever had to manage the process of cutting costs and managing layoffs? If so, what did that teach you about courage and compassion?

Another way to explore this question is to consider the best-performing bosses and colleagues you have had. How did they approach major initiatives? What did they do to create momentum and deliver results? How did they think about getting the job done *now* while building capacity for *next time*? Conversely, think about the leaders you have encountered who took a system or a culture that was humming and managed to ruin it. What did you learn *not* to do? What were some critical lessons?

Could you distill these insights into a few guidelines to help a rookie leader get off to a strong start on a major initiative and build momentum?

Move from Prototype to Prime Time

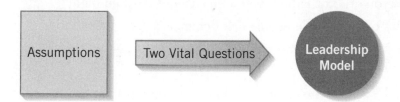

The value of prototyping is that it allows you to take your best ideas and make them tangible. When you do so, the secret is to try out a lot of ideas quickly, discard what doesn't work, and do it again. By creating a prototype of your leadership model, you will have something tangible you can react to and refine until it is clear, coherent, and effective. The aim is to develop a model that you can draw on the back of a napkin while explaining your leadership approach to someone else. (The Campbell Leadership Model, which you have seen earlier in this chapter, is one example; for other examples, please visit www.conantleadership.com.)

Think About Your Insights

To start developing your prototype, reflect on the assertive, adaptive, and integrative points of view and the way you responded to the two vital questions. Jot down your insights (a stack of Post-it notes is helpful for this activity). Don't stop to think too much at this point—write down whatever occurs to you. Your notes might include things like "Keep score real-time," "If you are not failing, you aren't trying hard enough," "Unreasonable people drive change," "Help *them* do it," "Transparent and truthful," "Swagger is a good thing," or "Trust them."

Once you've written down everything that occurs to you, sort your thoughts and ideas into clusters. Some might deal with relationships while others focus on results; some might concern people's character and others, their competencies; some may stress the need for stability and others the importance of change. Play around with the clusters until the categories seem clear to you.

Create a Prototype

Next, step back and think about how the ideas are connected. This step is critical, because otherwise you are likely to end up with just a *list* instead of a logical *set* of ideas. The clusters might build on one another as in a hierarchy. They might overlap as in a Venn diagram. They might be connected in a way that is circular, simultaneous, or spiraling. They may even be expressed as a formula. Have some fun and play around with different possibilities.

When you have a good understanding of how your ideas are connected, quickly draw several rough prototypes of your leadership model. When you finish one, look at it and notice what you like. Then draw another, and another, until you have something that makes sense to you.

Once you have come up with a prototype that you think accurately expresses your own unique approach to leadership, see whether you can explain it to someone else. Grab someone you are comfortable with, such as a friend, your spouse, or a colleague, and take five or ten minutes to walk him or her through your model. You might feel hesitant and awkward the first time you do this, so do it with several people. If at this stage things are not flowing well, go back and create a few more prototypes until it all comes together.

Get Ready for Prime Time

When you feel confident that you can explain your model clearly, select one or two other people, such as a mentor or a colleague, whose opinions you respect. Ask those individuals to listen to your explanation and give you feedback: Does your model seem to be clear and coherent? Does it make sense to them? Are there any weaknesses in the ideas or the connections among them? Ask them to push you on this because, most of all, you want a model that works.

Once you are confident that your model is clear and coherent, you will be ready for prime time: to share it with your team, your boss, and other people you work with. Your model will make it easier for them to understand the way you think about leading people and change and *why* you make the calls you make in the moment. It will also make it easier for them to explain your ideas to others.

BE CONSISTENT *AND* FLEXIBLE

Once you have a solid model, you need to execute it consistently. Dieters who fail to lose weight often lack the discipline to stick to their weight-loss model. It must be a bad model, they think, so they abandon it and try another, often with the same poor results. In the same way, many leaders lack the discipline to implement their leadership models fully. Unhappy with the results, they drop the model and start shopping for another management idea. Using your head means you become disciplined in both your thinking *and* your implementation.

There are, of course, times when you do need to make adjustments to your model. As you continue your study of leadership and gain more experience as a leader, you will develop an even better understanding of human nature and the nature of change, and this understanding may lead to changes in your leadership model. For example, if you created the model during an economic expansion, you may find that it doesn't hold up when the economy contracts. Or if you have taken on new responsibilities, you may need to adjust from leading an all-Australian team to one in which half the team is Chinese.

Still another reason to adjust your model is that you want to anticipate the future. As the speed, complexities, expectations, and accountabilities continue to escalate, you will need better and faster ways to engage people and accelerate the pace of change. How might you need to lead differently in the future? If your aspiration is to lead a large organization ten or twenty years from now, this is the new frontier.

THE POINT IS . . .

Douglas McGregor, a pioneer in management theory, was exasperated by the sloppiness of many leaders' thinking, pointing out that most of them lack the mental discipline we would expect from an engineer. A hydroelectrical engineer, for example, must have an understanding of *the nature of water* in order to build a dam. Were he to construct a dam that required water to run uphill, no one would blame the water for refusing to cooperate. They would put the responsibility exactly where it belonged—with the incompetent engineer.

Likewise, leaders must understand *human nature and the nature of change* in order to lead effectively. Yet when employees don't respond to change initiatives as expected, managers get away with comments like "People resist change." Well, of course they do! At least most do, unless they have a compelling reason to make the change. A good model must account for such resistance and anticipate how to overcome it.

One reason leaders become exasperated is that many of them don't accept that it takes time to create deep and sustainable change. It is as if, refusing to believe that it takes women nine months to carry a baby to term, they put nine women in a room 24/7 and tell them to deliver in one month. Then, when that doesn't work, they wonder, "What if we gave the women a bigger bonus or allowed them to bring their pets to work? Might it work then?"

The secret to using your energy and resources wisely is to work *with*, not against, the nature of things. That doesn't mean you shouldn't experiment. In fact, it is healthy to test some wild ideas, because they are the ones that will create breakthrough leadership solutions. And, let's face it, there is a lot of room for improvement. Today the average leader gets only a C– when it comes to people giving the very best of themselves.[2]

---

[2] Towers Watson, *Towers Watson 2010 Global Workforce Study*, conducted in twenty-two markets with more than twenty thousand employees. The report showed that only 21 percent of employees were engaged, 42 percent were enrolled, and 38 percent were either disenchanted or actively disengaged. (Percentages do not add up to 100 due to rounding.)

But before you roll out an enticing new program, you should experiment: do a test or run a pilot, and then look at the data. If people don't behave as you expected them to, instead of getting irritated with them, get curious. Ask yourself, *Isn't that interesting? I wonder why*, and then look for a more useful explanation for how the world works.

Einstein once observed that the person who "can no longer wonder, no longer feel amazement, is as good as dead."[3] To be fully alive in the way you lead, you need to be curious, ask good questions, and find the approach that works for you in your unique culture and context.

In other words, make a commitment to inquiry.

[3] Albert Einstein, *The World As I See It* (New York: Philosophical Library, 1949), p. 5. (Essay text available at: http://being.publicradio.org/programs/einsteinsethics/einstein-theworldasiseeit.shtml.)

4

Use Your Heart

THE COMMITMENT
TO REFLECTION

Some leaders say, "It's not personal; it's just business."
Don't buy it! What these leaders mean is that they believe
that to show strength, you need to be tough-minded
and tough-hearted. But the opposite is the case. What
takes real courage is to make your work intensely
personal: to care about your work and about the people
you work with. We believe that when you use your
heart, you will make better judgments concerning *the
issue*; you will make stronger connections with *the other
people*; and you will develop your personal authority as *a
leader*.

LEAD WITH YOUR HEAD *AND* YOUR HEART

Some of the decisions you need to make in a TouchPoint are clear-cut. You simply get the best data available, do the analysis, and make the call. In most cases, though, you need to consider more than the numbers. There are even times when the numbers reveal one course of action to be the *smart* thing to do, yet you know it is not the *right* thing to do. In such cases, you need to trust your intuition and connect to your principles. You need to use both your head *and* your heart to make a wise decision.

Let's consider a real-life scenario in which a leader had to do just that. John (not his real name) had recently taken a position as VP of a supply chain in a multinational firm. After John had been in the job for four months, a worker at one of the company's plants he was responsible for died suddenly. Although the death might have been caused by a work-related accident, it was most likely the result of a severe and chronic medical condition.

Shortly after the accident, John participated in a conference call with the CFO and the VP responsible for the company's insurance policies. The person from the insurance department explained that, because there was some legitimate question about the cause of death, they had the option to deny the worker's compensation claim. "If we deny the claim," she said, "the company can avoid paying the $1 million deductible." Budgets were tight, and $1 million was a significant amount of money.

Logically, it made sense to fight the claim. What would you have done?

To John, who had been a plant manager earlier in his career, this was not a matter of logic; it was a matter of principle. He said, "Each day, that plant manager has to be able to look his people in the eye. Every Sunday, he has to go to church and see this man's wife. We have to pay." The CFO backed him up. The word soon got out as the safety managers from the plant told their colleagues at the other sites about the decision. As a result, when John later visited other factories, the employees would stop him and thank him for doing the right thing. By leading with his heart at a critical moment, he had earned their trust and benefited from the exponential effect of a TouchPoint.

Leading with heart doesn't mean you always decide in favor of the individual. It just means that when you need to make a tough-minded decision, you are acutely aware of how it will affect the people involved. That awareness is what can make it so difficult for leaders to give a tough performance review.

That was the situation Doug was facing at the end of one fiscal year. The economy had been extremely difficult, and on top of that he had been in a very serious automobile accident. For months his team had covered for him. They had done a great job and largely delivered or overdelivered against the original expectations. But when he and the board took a hard look, the team's performance was below average relative to the rest of their peer group.

"The fact is that we could have done better, and we should have done better," Doug thought. What troubled him the most was that the leaders on his team were planning to give their staffs an above-average rating, reflecting their performance against the original expectations despite their below-average performance relative to their peer group. "I was really conflicted. While I was laid up in the hospital, they were working so hard to get our company through this rough patch. And they did! And now I may be returning the favor by saying, 'Thank you very much; your performance was good, but it wasn't good enough.' Ultimately, in my opinion, we should have done better."

How do you think you would have handled this situation? Here's what Doug decided. After two weeks of deliberation, he gave himself and the ten members of his immediate team the same below-average performance rating. He wanted to send a really strong message, and by personally dealing with his team, he was exponentially recalibrating the conversations that would be held across the organization. By sending such a powerful signal, everyone would know that they needed to bring their performance up a notch.

Of course, John's and Doug's decisions were more important and far reaching than most of the calls leaders make in the course of a day. But even when making minor decisions, you want to use your heart. For example, in a brief TouchPoint you may need to decide whether to start an off-site meeting on a Monday or a Tuesday, a decision that determines whether people get to spend Sunday at home instead of in an airport. Or you may need to revisit a project deadline in a situation where keeping your commitment means everyone on your team will need to work 24/7 all next week, and not keeping it means letting down colleagues who have arranged their schedules around the handoff. Each day, dozens of such minor decisions affect the trust people have in their leader, the pride they take in working for the team, and the strength of their commitment. That is why, in even the smallest of moments, you want to use both your head *and* your heart.

To make genuine connections with other people, you need to bring more than information and experience to the interaction—you need to bring yourself. Today's employees are sophisticated consumers of media and communications, and they can smell spin a mile away. Before they choose to engage fully, they want to see more than a company face and hear more than corporate platitudes. They want to meet real people.

Sadly, many leaders hold back essential aspects of who they are. They hide their heart instead of showing it. Consequently, they end up with transactional relationships and lukewarm commitments. You can do better than that.

ANSWER THE QUESTIONS OF THE HEART

In the previous chapter, you considered two questions that encouraged you to look at the way the *world* works. Now we ask you to reflect on the way *you* work. To that end, we will share the three questions of the heart that we use with the participants in the CEO Institute:

1. Why do I choose to lead?
2. What is my code?
3. How well do I walk the talk?

The leaders in the CEO Institute report that answering these questions has made them more grounded, more effective, and more confident:

"I originally thought I had to be the kind of leader everyone
 expected me to be, but now I'm finding my own path."
"When I stopped worrying about what others wanted me to
 be, I became so much more effective."
"Knowing my purpose gave me strength."
"Becoming more comfortable in my own skin gave me more
 confidence. After that things just started to happen. I
 began to get a lot more recognition and more opportunities."

We invite you to make time for these questions so you can experience similar gains in your ability to lead.

Why Do I Choose to Lead?

All too often, people become leaders because doing so was the next logical step in their careers. They know what they want to *get* from their position (such as a new challenge, more influence, more prestige, or better pay), but many are vague about what they want to *give*. Many have a good *reason* to lead, but they are tentative about their *purpose*. Yet leadership is hard work. Without a clear purpose, is being a leader really worth the long hours, the endless meetings, the wrangling over forecasts and budgets, the reports, the grumbling, and the travel? Is it really worth devoting more of your waking hours to work, or to thinking about work, than to anything else? Is that really the way you want to spend your life?

Knowing *why* you want to lead gives you a well of energy to draw on that is deeper than merely finding meaning in your work. For example, you may be marketing latex gloves, and find meaning in the fact that you are helping prevent the spread of infectious diseases. But that doesn't necessarily mean that the work itself is personally fulfilling. Meaning is a matter of context, of understanding how your work adds value to someone, somewhere. Purpose, in contrast, is profoundly personal. It is about finding your place in the larger scheme of things; it is about loving what you do; it is about feeling, "Yes, this is what I was meant to do!"

The challenge is that most of us don't take the time to connect to our passion and purpose. And when we do, we struggle to find the words to express it. Although we are well trained in the language of reason, we don't have the words to express what is in our hearts. To communicate such thoughts, we enter the realm of poets and songwriters, playwrights and philosophers.

The quest, in the words of the poet Pamela Vaull Starr, is to

Reach high, for stars lie hidden in your soul.
Dream deep, for every dream precedes the goal.

When dealing with dreams, however, you want to remember that there is a difference between being a daydreamer and a dreamer of the day. Daydreamers merely seek to escape reality, whereas "the dreamers of the day... act their dreams with open eyes, to make it possible."[1] They are the ones who recognize that we live in an imperfect world, yet they get up each day and do their part to make it better.

What is your dream? What is the work that you feel called to do?

In our experience, those who are called to leadership really care about the people on their team and could talk for hours about each of them: what has shaped them, how they have developed, and what it will take for each person to grow into his or her potential. They can talk about the team's dynamics and their plans for making the team even stronger. To them, leading people is much more than a job.

[1] T. E. Lawrence, *Seven Pillars of Wisdom* (Ware, England: Wordsworth, 1997), p. 7. (Original work published 1922)

One way to detect your dream is to think about the leaders who have inspired you. In Doug's case, one of his many role models is Teddy Roosevelt, and to this day he can cite the words from a famous speech Roosevelt gave back in 1910: "[T]he credit belongs to the man who is actually in the arena; whose face is marred by dust and sweat and blood; who strives valiantly; who errs and comes up short again and again; who knows the enthusiasm, the great devotions, and spends himself in a worthy cause..."

These words, along with many others, have helped Doug find his purpose in the corporate arena. His cause has been to take tired, toxic cultures and turn them around. His passion has been *to build world-class organizations that defy the critics and thrive in the face of adversity.* That is the sense of purpose he chooses to bring to his work. Why do *you* choose to lead?

If you have trouble answering the question, think about this: it may be that you do not really *want* to lead. You might not want to be accountable for so many people's performance. Yes, you may want to have more influence, but maybe your way of influencing others is as a star performer, a specialist, or an expert in your chosen field.

After a few years as a leader, that was the conclusion Mette came to. She found that although being a leader was *good* work, it just wasn't *her* work. She was forty-two before she realized that what she really loved to do was help other leaders be more authentic and alive in their work, so that they could create workplaces where people would thrive and give the very best of themselves. In her experience, when leaders love what they do, they become superb at doing it, which enriches the lives of everyone around them. Conversely, when they are bad at it, they do great damage. With each leader she influences, she has a positive impact on the lives of hundreds, if not thousands, of other people. That is her purpose, her passion.

What Is My Code?

Every leader needs a code to live by, a set of principles that provides an underlying consistency in every Touch-Point. Without that consistency, you might come across as being a chameleon-like leader. When you have clear principles, people know what you stand for and how you choose to walk in the world.

Can you think of a TouchPoint in which you took a principled stance, even though it might have been a difficult decision, even a career-limiting move? What did it feel like when you acted with integrity, when you did what you felt was the right thing to do? Those TouchPoints can give you a stronger sense of who you are. They can make you feel honorable, battle hardened, and worthy of people's respect. As John discovered when he decided to pay the worker's compensation claim, when you act with integrity to the point of taking a stand that is inconvenient, risky, or against your own interest, you are showing people that you can be trusted.

Your code is based on the principles you believe in and captures what to you is the right thing to do. When you live your code, you have a good conscience; when you violate it, you disappoint yourself. There are many TouchPoints during which you won't feel like doing the right thing, especially when you feel unfairly treated or betrayed. These are the times when it is useful to be guided by a clear code and to spend time with people who bring out the best in you.

Doug is forever grateful to Neil McKenna for helping him find his code and raise his sights. Doug started his career at General Mills. After having devoted ten years of his life to the company, the subsidiary he worked for was spun off, and the new owners decided to eliminate his position. One morning, Doug was simply called into the office, asked to pack his things, and told to be out of the building by noon. Doug remembers the moment as if it were yesterday: "Ten years of my work life were over just like that! And the guy charged with letting me go couldn't even look me in the eye." He went home that day to his wife, two small children, and a very large mortgage.

Fortunately, before he left the office, Doug was put in touch with an outplacement specialist, a crusty New Englander who answered his phone, "Neil McKenna, how can I help?" When Neil heard what had happened, one of the things he asked Doug to do was to take a couple of days to reflect on his family history and then to come in to his office.

When Doug met with Neil a few days later, he was feeling conflicted by how to handle a number of decisions relating to his separation from the company. Neil listened for a while and then asked, "What would your grandfather do?" Doug didn't hesitate: "He'd take the high ground." Suddenly Doug knew in his heart what he needed to do. Instead of nitpicking every minor decision, he decided to trust that the company would deal with him fairly during the separation process. And the company did.

As in Doug's case, much of what we consider to be "the right thing to do" was encoded very early in life. Even before first grade, we knew how to treat the kids who were smaller than we were, how to deal with bullies, how to share, and what it meant to be responsible. Our code continued to evolve over the years as a teacher taught us that high standards were a sign of ethics, a coach helped us learn what it means to be a real team player, or a boss imparted her code about what it means to take full responsibility for a job.

As we grow older, we begin to examine the things we were told to believe, and to develop our own answers. For example, you might have been raised with the maxim, "Winning isn't everything; it's the only thing," only to realize at some point in your life that winning at all costs leaves a bad taste in your mouth. Your code evolved as you discovered that what you really believe in is "winning with integrity." Now, when you carry that code with you into TouchPoint after TouchPoint, the people on your team know that you expect them to compete not by backstabbing or undermining others but by pushing themselves and becoming the absolute best that they can be.

Through personal reflection, you can start to capture the principles you choose to live by.

Think about a time when you took a stand. Why did you do it? What was the principle involved? How did it make you feel? What about a time when you didn't take a stand but felt that you should have? What principles were you ignoring? What were the consequences?

Having worked with thousands of leaders over the past thirty years, we have found that those who have achieved a high level of mastery seek to serve their organization and their team before their own careers. In military parlance, the code is "First the mission, second the team, and then oneself."

It's not always easy to apply your code in the face of differing circumstances, however. For example, when you are part of a multicultural team, you may discover quite different views of what it means to live with honor. As a leader, you must be open to other such interpretations. But let's be clear that this is not the same as moral relativism. It just means that instead of acting self-righteously, you ask yourself, *What's the most just, the most truthful, the most ethical thing to do in this particular situation?*

That's a question that Clayton (not his real name), the head of a $1 billion business unit, needed to answer when he moved from Jamaica to the United States. Clayton's code is centered around a profound respect for other people. In Jamaica, one of the ways you show respect is to stay in a conversation until it has run its natural course. Thus Clayton felt that it was right to remain in a conversation until it was over, even when that would make him late for his next meeting.

But Clayton discovered that attitudes toward being late are different in the United States than they are in Jamaica. At first, he paid little attention to the feedback he was getting about being late—in his culture, being late was no big deal. But soon he realized that his new colleagues felt that being late was disrespectful. His culture had taught him one thing, but his new environment required something else. He didn't change his code, but to honor it by respecting others, he learned that he sometimes needed to cut a TouchPoint short for him to make it to another appointment on time.

Having a code helps you keep your perspective when you are doing well and take the high ground in times of adversity. Your code is especially important when you are tempted to take a few shortcuts to success. Sadly, interviews with remarkably accomplished professionals show that many of them believe they can't afford to be principled.[2] They are convinced that their peers are cutting corners, so to compete they feel they need to do the same. They rationalize that once they get to the top, then they will do the right thing. But that is a flawed premise, because over time you become that which you repeatedly do—when you take shortcuts to success, you become the type of person who takes shortcuts.

For you as a leader, the stakes are high, because the code you live by reflects on your team, your unit, and your company. Mette was reminded of that point when, at the age of eighteen, she left her home in Denmark to work in England. As they said their good-byes, Mette's father put his hand on her shoulder and said with great sincerity, "Remember you are an ambassador for your country. Whatever you do will reflect on your fellow Danes." That was a big message packed into a small moment.

As a leader, you are the ambassador for your team. Serving the team well gives you the right to "put your hand on their shoulder" and remind your team members to do the same.

How Well Do I Walk the Talk?

Each TouchPoint is a small test: You say you want people to be candid, but do you really want to hear what they have to

[2] Wendy Fischman, Becca Solomon, Deborah Schutte, and Howard Gardner, *Making Good: How Young People Cope with Moral Dilemmas at Work* (Cambridge, MA: Harvard University Press, 2004).

say? You say you want them to run with the ball, but do you really let them? When you "walk the talk," people find you more credible. Then, if you stumble, they pause to see what you will do next. If you get back up and promise to do better, they cut you some slack; and if you keep your promise, they begin to trust you. As a leader, your goal is to walk the talk in TouchPoint after TouchPoint.

How well do you walk the talk? Be honest with yourself, and keep in mind that it's common for people to think that they are doing better than they actually are. Marshall Goldsmith, coach to many of the world's leading CEOs and author of *What Got You Here Won't Get You There*, has asked over fifty thousand people how they rate themselves compared to their peers. It turns out that about 70 percent rate themselves as being in the top 10 percent.[3] Well, we all know that this is just not possible mathematically. How do we explain such self-ratings? The answer is that people tend to listen to the feedback that confirms the way they already see themselves and to ignore the rest. Therefore, if you really want to improve, you need some ways of taking a clear-eyed look at yourself. You need strategies for keeping yourself honest. In the words of the philosopher Ralph Waldo Emerson,

[3] Marshall Goldsmith, "The Success Delusion," *Conference Board Review*, January-February 2007. (Available at www.marshallgoldsmithlibrary.com/cim /articles_display.php?aid=321)

"Whatever games are played with us, we must play no games with ourselves."[4]

Let's say your code includes "honesty" and "respect," and you see yourself as someone who talks straight and pays attention when others talk. Okay, that is what you *say* is important, but is it what other people *see* you do? "Well, of course!" you may think to yourself. "I don't lie or deceive people, nor do I cut them off, and I certainly never belittle anyone." So what you are saying is that you don't *violate* your code. But do you *live* it?

Our biggest challenge lies in what Stephen M. R. Covey, author of *The Speed of Trust*, calls *counterfeit behaviors*. You may *say* you value straight talk, but when you are in a TouchPoint, do people *see* you beat around the bush, withhold information, or spin the facts? You may be fully present during meetings when your own team members speak, but when a member of someone else's team gets up to talk, do you check your smartphone and begin to answer messages?

The easiest way to keep yourself honest is to become clear-eyed about how you use one of your most important resources: your time. A more data-driven way is to get unfiltered 360-degree feedback on your behavior. Yet another way is to find a couple of trusted advisers who care

[4]Ralph Waldo Emerson, "Illusions," *Atlantic Monthly 1*, no. 1 (1857). (Available at www.theatlantic.com/past/docs/issues/1857nov/emersonillusions.htm)

about your success and will be candid with you. Let's look more closely at each of those strategies.

Make Time for What You Say Is Important.

Doug believes that leaders must develop the people around them, but what does his calendar show? When it comes to the CEO Institute, a two-year program, he has blocked out time in his schedule for five off-site sessions (twelve days for each group) and set aside time for twenty one-hour coaching conversations. In addition, he allocates time to read and respond to one hundred Leadership Letters (each participant writes a letter capturing his or her insights and reflections after each session). Of course it is easy to schedule something; the hard part is to do it. In Doug's case, the participants saw him honor his commitments every time. Even when he was finalizing the sale of the Godiva chocolate company, he was there. Most touching, he also cofacilitated when he was recovering from his car accident and able to attend for only a few hours each day.

How tenacious are you about making time for the things that matter most? How might you make better time choices?

Here is how one leader did it. When Joe was promoted to chief information officer for a Fortune 500 firm, he knew that the demands on his time would multiply dramatically. He wanted to make sure he would invest his time at work in the right things; he also wanted to get home for dinner and have enough time for mountain biking and snowboarding.

Joe's colleague Phil said, "I'll keep you honest." Joe created a set of criteria and a list of priorities, and they set up a weekly routine. Each Sunday night, Joe would plan his week and send Phil the schedule. The next morning they would do a quick huddle: Did the activities really meet the criteria? Were the priorities clear? Was he allowing time between TouchPoints to recharge his batteries? Buffer time for surprises? Before long, Joe became acutely aware of how he allocated his time and was able to invest it wisely.

Get Feedback.

Another excellent way to keep yourself honest is to gather some data on how you are doing. Instruments such as 360-degree profiles are great tools for helping you learn and grow as a leader. It's quite a reality check when you find that on an important behavior, you rated yourself 80 percent effective, whereas others gave you only 50 percent.

There are many such instruments to choose from. When dealing with intact teams, Mette finds the Inventory of Leadership Styles from the Hay Group to be an eye-opener. Most leaders like to think of themselves as acing the Visionary style, but their direct reports tend to experience them as Pacesetters. When it comes to

TouchPoints, this difference is enormous: a leader who uses the Visionary style takes time to frame the issue in relation to the team's strategy or to explain the standards; in contrast, the Pacesetting style characterizes a leader who is too impatient to listen and too rushed to explain things.[5]

Have a Trusted Adviser.

You may want to cultivate good relationships with a mentor, a former boss, a colleague, or a coach. The key is to find someone who can see your potential, who cares about your success, and who will be honest with you. The challenge for many leaders is that the higher up they go, the more oblique people become about giving them feedback. You need someone you trust to give it to you straight.

A good time for such a heart-to-heart conversation is at the end of each quarter. Together you can explore such questions as How did you do with the numbers? How is your energy? How committed is the team? Where have you stumbled, and how did you regain your stride? How are things at home? Is the pace sustainable? One challenge for many leaders is to be confident without becoming arrogant, and the only person who can guide you here is a trusted adviser.

[5]Daniel Goleman, "Leadership That Gets Results," *Harvard Business Review*, March-April 2000, pp. 78–90.

THE POINT IS . . .

Beyond the three questions of the heart, leaders often struggle with a fourth question, which is about accountability. They wonder whether their first loyalty should be to the customers, the shareholders, the employees, or the community.

The reality is that you have many constituents, and they are all important. But Shakespeare had it right: "To thy own self be true." At the end of the day, you have to be able to look at yourself in the mirror. *First and foremost, you are accountable to yourself.* That, of course, requires you to know yourself.

To be true to yourself, continue the process of self-discovery by answering the questions "Why do I choose to lead?" and "What is my code?" at ever deeper levels. A strong connection to your purpose and principles can function as your personal GPS, an inner guidance system that you can refer to in any TouchPoint. This connection provides an inner strength, which lets you continuously extend yourself and build healthy relationships.

To reinforce the insights you gain by asking those questions, start each day with something that inspires you: a poem, a passage from a book, or a song that gives you a lift. During the day, try to spend time with people who bring out the best in you. End the day by asking yourself, *How well did I walk the talk today? What could I have done better?*

It takes time to grow into your full stature as a leader, and most people don't reach it until midcareer. But when they do, as the journalist Dave Halberstam so aptly observed, you can hear it in their tone of voice and sense it in their feeling for command; they become people you don't want to fail.[6] This aura is not the same as being arrogant or charismatic, far from it. Instead, it comes from the genuine sense of purpose and inner confidence you gain when you have the heart of a leader.

[6]David Halberstam, "The Greatness That Cannot Be Taught," *Fast Company*, September 2004, p. 65.

5
Use Your Hands

●

THE COMMITMENT
TO PRACTICE

*T*ouchPoints are intensely practical, because each one deals with real people and real issues and does so in real time. Therefore, it is not enough to be clear-headed and clear-hearted in a TouchPoint; you must also be clearly competent. Developing the skills so that you can be proficient in TouchPoint after TouchPoint requires continuous practice.

When Mette runs into graduates from the CEO Institute, she always asks, "What's become clear since you graduated?" When she recently posed that question to Ed, the general manager of a business unit with twenty-five hundred employees, he laughed and replied, "Being a leader is really, really hard!" He added, "I have learned that there is almost never a day when I don't go home feeling that I could have done better. And on that occasional day where I say to myself, 'I really did get it right today,' that's the day I don't get it right at home."

Ed is right: becoming competent in TouchPoint after TouchPoint is really, really hard. Like Ed, the best leaders are always pushing themselves. They are constantly looking to increase their TouchPoint ratio of "That went well" to "I blew it." And they know that to do so, they need to practice.

THE POWER OF PRACTICE

If you were starting college today and wanted to succeed in the global workplace, what would you study? Would the best career move be to excel in Mandarin, digital media, or something else? The fact is, we live in a complex, dynamic environment, and no one can predict with any accuracy what competencies people will need in twenty years. We just don't know.

As Charles Darwin observed, when the environment is changing rapidly, it is neither the strongest nor the most intelligent who survive—it is the ones who are most adaptable. Thus, the fittest leaders are those most capable of learning. That is why authors like Thomas Friedman (*Hot, Flat, and Crowded*) stress that the most important competence today is *learning how to learn*.

Real learning takes place at the edge of your current abilities. Whether you are motivated by a desire to be the best among your peers or by an inner vision of what is possible, you learn faster when you have a genuine passion for the topic and a fierce commitment to practice. Consider Wayne Gretzky, who many Canadians believe was the greatest hockey player ever. Gretzky was not the strongest player, nor was he the fastest on the ice. His forte was, in his own words, the ability to "skate to where the puck is going to be."

Most people saw Gretzky's amazing skill as an innate talent, but the reality was that he had worked at it from childhood. As a boy, when he was watching hockey on TV, his father would give him pen and paper and ask him to trace the movement of the puck. During breaks, the two of them would then look at his drawings and analyze the pattern. It was a simple practice, but by doing it over and over again, Gretzky developed an incredible sense of the situation, a real instinct for the game.

Likewise it takes a lot of training to be fully present to someone else's needs in a TouchPoint. Doug experienced this firsthand when he was in the hospital recovering from his accident. All his nurses would follow the same protocol when they entered the room. "Every nurse who came in would ask, 'How is your pain?' and I'd have to rate it on a 1-to-10 scale. As I did, they were really paying attention to me. They genuinely wanted to know how I was doing, so they could help.

"But sometimes the less experienced nurses would come through. They would ask the same question, 'How is your pain?' but they seemed to be very anxious about what I was going to say. It was as if they weren't sure they could deal with the answer. Their lack of experience made it feel as if that moment wasn't about me; it was about them."

Like Gretzky, leaders need to do drills in order to become competent; and like the nurses, they need to train in order to gain real confidence. Only by putting in the hours of practice can you become capable, confident, and coolheaded in the moment.

A SHARED UNDERSTANDING

TouchPoints are all about communication. To handle whatever might be thrown at you in the moment, you need to be incredibly skilled at understanding what others are saying and also at making yourself understood.

But what does *communication* really mean? When leaders say, "What I have learned is that you need to communicate, communicate, communicate!" they often mean they need to broadcast their message more often and at stronger frequencies. Communication is not about continuously transmitting your point of view like a radio signal, however. That is too narrow a sense of the word. *Communication* comes from the Latin word *communis*. It's about having something in common. In a TouchPoint, that means having a shared understanding of where we are now, where we want to go, and how we will get there.

That kind of communication requires both clear speaking *and* careful listening.

The challenge for leaders is that, because they are so visible and have the power to affect people's lives, the way they communicate in a TouchPoint can have unintended consequences. That was something that became clear to Ed on a particularly demanding day.

Ed was dealing with several pressing business issues and getting ready for a very important presentation to the CEO on a new growth plan for his division. He had asked Carol, the head of innovation, to take the lead on the plan. He realized that the assignment was a stretch for her, but he was confident she could handle it.

At the end of the day, Carol came by Ed's office wanting to talk about the plan. "My expectation was that she would have put some words on paper so we would have something to look at together," he said. But it turned out that Carol was not that far along on the plan. "I became very frustrated and prodded her to give me something I could react to. I was really disappointed and irritated that she hadn't figured it out, and she could tell.

"I said, 'Carol it looks like we are a long way from where we need to be, and I don't have time to deal with it right now.' As soon as the words tumbled out, I saw this look on her face, and her shoulders slumped. I knew I had made a huge mistake."

Ed regrets what happened. Carol had come to him with a genuine request for help, and he not only failed to give her any help but also spoke to her in a way that undermined her confidence. Although he went out of his way to apologize later that evening and again the next day, he knew that it would take time for her to regain her self-assurance. Confidence can be an incredibly fragile thing.

In Ed's case, the problem was amplified by the fact that he had only been in the position for four months, and he and Carol did not yet know each other well. They had not had time to build the level of trust that is so important to clear communication.

Build Relationships

Communication takes place in the relationship between two or more people, so the faster you can build relationships, the easier the communication becomes. But to make real connections, you need to see the others as *people* instead of as subordinates, followers, or hired guns. Or, when influencing up, you need to look beyond "the suit," the "boss," or the "VP" and see the other *person* in that TouchPoint. Every interaction involves human beings who have their own priorities, anxieties, hopes, and dreams.

To build relationships, you need to take the time to talk to people. Get to know them. Learn their stories. Listen for what drives them, what they care about, what they take pride in, and what concerns them. We all have a tendency to assume that other people are motivated by the same things that motivate us. But we're all different. You will be much better at influencing others and gaining their commitment when you know what *they* value.

To Mark, head of the Asia Pacific region for a multinational firm, it came as a revelation that what motivated other people was often different from what motivated him. During an off-site strategy session, the facilitator asked each person on Mark's team what he or she really came to work for. As Mark listened to people's responses, he remembers thinking, "Holy cow! I had no idea *that* could be the reason someone comes to work every day." It soon became obvious that just because *he* got a kick out of smashing earnings and sales targets, that was not enough for some others.

Mark was quick to build on that insight. He created a practice that he called *purposeful open questions.* For example, he might open a casual conversation by sharing his passion for leadership, talking about why he loved what he did, and then turn to the other person and say, "Tell me your thing." What Mark learned during those TouchPoints helped him look for stretch assignments that matched each person's talent and interests.

Building relationships also helps you get to know people's strengths and uncover their potential. Pam, the head of talent development for a global training and development firm, had eight directors reporting to her. When the book *Now, Discover Your Strengths,* by Marcus Buckingham and Donald Clifton, was published, she told her team that she would buy everyone a copy, providing they would create a chart with their own photo, name, and top five strengths, and allow her to put the charts on her office wall where everyone could see them. The directors agreed.

Once the charts had been posted, Pam began each staff meeting by asking one of the directors to give examples of how he or she had seen another director's strengths at play. In addition, whenever a task or a project needed to be assigned, Pam would say, "Let's look at our charts. Who has the strengths to help with what we are about to do?" People soon felt confident that their own strengths would be called on and that they were being acknowledged for being themselves.

Such small practices allow you to tap into the magic of each moment and release the power and potential of a TouchPoint.

Declare Yourself

In addition to listening to other people's stories and uncovering their strengths, leaders need to do what Mark does: be transparent about who *they* are. Tell people why you choose to lead and the code you choose to live by. Let them know where you are struggling and what they can do to help.

When you first begin the practice of speaking from the heart, it can feel awkward and uncomfortable, because telling others what you care about can make you feel vulnerable. Yet remember the story from Chapter One of Lisa, the VP who led an innovation team? By letting her colleague know who she was, she created a space for a heart-to-heart conversation that led to a stronger working relationship. We call this *declaring yourself.*

Declaring yourself takes practice. In the CEO Institute, after leaders have had two days of reflection, we ask them to sit in small groups and give words to what is in their hearts. For many of them, this is the first time they have told their colleagues about their passion for leadership and the code they seek to live by.

Afterwards, the group offers feedback: Did what they hear resonate with how they previously experienced the person? Did it feel genuine? Did it sound true? That conversation leads to a palpable shift in the quality of the relationships. This is the morning the participants become a true community of learners, deeply committed to one another's growth.

If you feel uncomfortable about declaring yourself to your team, create your own practice. Sit with a loved one, a good friend, or a coach. Explain why you choose to lead and talk about your passion and your purpose. Then try again, this time with a colleague or a couple of team members. As your confidence grows, so will the strength of the connections.

LEAD WITH LISTENING

Listening is one of the most amazingly efficient things you can do as a leader. But listening can be very hard to do. One reason is that most leaders have a bias for action, and when they are listening, it does not feel as though they are *doing* anything. Listening is even more difficult in today's interruption age, when we have become so accustomed to the constant stimulation that many of us have even developed ADT ("attention deficit traits"). Consequently, after trying to pay attention for a couple of minutes, your mind starts drifting, your fingers start twitching, and you reach for your PDA.

But in a TouchPoint, listening with your head and with your heart is critical if you are to gain a good understanding of the issue. Without that understanding, you can easily waste everyone's time by solving the wrong problem or by merely addressing a symptom, not the underlying disease.

The challenge for many leaders is that when they have some familiarity with an issue, they assume that they know what the other people are going to say. They listen for a minute or two and then jump in, ready with a "fix," before they understand what's really going on. They waste not only the chance to get it right the first time but also opportunities to learn from people who may have a much better understanding of an aspect of their organization than they do.

To use people's time and energy wisely, you want to listen with your head for the evidence, listen with your heart for the energy, and listen exponentially to all the other voices that touch the issue.

Listen with Your Head

Listening with your head means listening for the *evidence*—facts and figures, actions, events, and conversations—that led to the current TouchPoint.

Most TouchPoints deal with quick updates and straightforward tactical issues; in those interactions, you simply get the information, find out what the other person needs, and provide it.

But when the issue is more complex, you need to give the other people more time to describe the situation. To make sure you stay with them on their agenda instead of hijacking it, here is a small practice you can try. Whenever someone is seeking to explain something to you and you feel a question or piece of advice bubbling up, bite your tongue! Then, before you open your mouth, ask yourself, *How exactly will this comment be helpful to the others?*

In some cases, you may need to dive into the data to figure out what is going on. Even when dealing with subjective issues, such as an upset customer or an interpersonal conflict, take a reading of the order of magnitude by asking something like, "On a scale of 1 to 10, how bad is this situation?" Such understanding will enable you to better calibrate your response in the moment.

When dealing with complex issues, here is a practice that can help you understand what's really going on.

Instead of pretending that you understand or being concerned about asking a stupid question, ask the other people what they mean. Say, "I don't understand. Could you explain that to me?" "Could you clarify that?" or "Please tell me more about that." Encourage the other people to fill in the gaps so that you can get a complete picture. Such questions help you dig deeper into the issue without taking over the agenda.

Listen with Your Heart

When you listen with your heart for the energy in a TouchPoint, you tune in to how the other people are feeling. You are curious about why people interpret the facts the way they do and how they feel about the situation. That means you pay attention not only to words but also to the facial expressions, tone of voice, and body language that reveal whether people feel excited, nervous, upset, unsure, committed, or confident.

An easy practice that can help you tune in to the feelings in a TouchPoint is to imagine the energy as being red, yellow, or green. It's like coming to a traffic light: you stop if it's red, slow down if it's yellow, or go on through if it's green. By remaining alert for the "traffic signal" in a TouchPoint, you can determine whether and how to proceed.

When the energy is red. We say the energy in a Touch-Point is red when people are testy or angry, when they become vocal about why your proposal won't work, or when they withdraw, avoid eye contact, and shut down. If you sense that this is taking place, stop and listen. Try to find out what's going on. If they are disagreeing with you or resisting a proposed course of action, try to understand their reasoning. Perhaps they are concerned that a decision you want to make will undermine something that they are doing. Perhaps you are touching on something that to them is a matter of principle. Although you may be tempted to simply overrule their concerns and go for compliance, beware. Compliance may get the job done today, but what about this person's desire to contribute tomorrow?

Sometimes the energy in a TouchPoint turns red because we are feeling red ourselves. Those are the times when we say something insensitive like, "Cry a river, build a bridge, and get over it." Or when we do something like what Mette's boss did when he said, "If you can't do it, I'll find a real man for the job." In these situations, you don't need to tune into other people's energy; you need to manage your own.

When the energy is yellow. In a TouchPoint, people may express doubt, keep questioning something, or seem hesitant or uncertain about how to handle the situation. When that happens, slow down and listen with your heart. Giving people a chance to express their concerns can help both you and them find more workable ways to address the issue.

Sometimes other people's energy changes from green ("Go") to yellow right in front of your eyes. This may happen because you are more intent on perfecting the solution than on maximizing their level of engagement. For example, someone might be excited about an idea. It is a good idea, yet you can't stop yourself from showing the other person how it could be better. But you need to be very careful, because the more you "improve," the less she is likely to feel that she still owns it. In such cases, ask yourself whether it is better to have a superb solution with a standard level of engagement, or a standard solution with an intense feeling of ownership.

When the energy is green. Green energy means that the way is open for you and the others to move on; the other people in the TouchPoint feel curious, engaged, confident, and keen to move forward. Green energy doesn't mean that you can stop listening, however. In fact, the more engaged the other people are, the more you might want to listen, because they will probably be eager to offer good ideas and take on the responsibility for implementing them.

We need to say a word here about tuning into other people's energy when you are working with multicultural teams. It can be difficult enough to pick up the energy in a TouchPoint when you are working with people you know well and who have a background similar to yours. But tuning in and responding to that energy when you are working with people from different cultures can present a special challenge. Even though most leaders are alert to these challenges when working with people from "exotic" backgrounds, they often miss the more subtle distinctions.

For example, Mette recently worked with an American-Danish company that created business software solutions for professional services firms. Although American and Danish cultures are alike in many ways, there are some interesting differences, one of which relates to power. Being one of the most egalitarian tribes in the world, the Danes show little overt respect for authority. Consequently, where an American may listen attentively to a boss's proposal, a Dane is likely to raise lots of questions and want to weigh in on every decision before being good to go. To a Danish team leader, this would be normal behavior, but to an American boss, it might be interpreted as a lack of respect. So when you sense that the energy is turning yellow, slow down and try to understand why.

Listen Exponentially

Just as every TouchPoint you engage in can potentially impact many people beyond those who are immediately involved, every conversation you have with an individual or a group has been triggered by many prior Touch-Points. To gain an accurate and complete understanding of what is really going on, you need to think about all the stakeholders and listen for all the voices that touch the issue, even those that are not present. That kind of listening demands extraordinary attention.

Here is a solid practice that you can use to get the full picture. When people schedule time to meet with you about an important issue, ask them to come prepared with the answers to a few diagnostic questions, such as "What is the problem?" "Whom does this problem affect and how?" "What are the behaviors that are contributing to the problem?" "What would logically explain why people behave in that way?" and so forth. Then begin the meeting by giving them eight to ten minutes to lay out their answers to the questions while you listen without interrupting.

You will be amazed by how much you can learn in such a short time if you let people speak. Be so alert to what they say that when they are done, you can summarize what you heard in a few succinct sentences. Then ask, "Did I get this right?" Once you have a good understanding of the issue and what contributed to it, you will be able to figure out how to deal with it.

A challenge many leaders have is that whereas employees are usually tuned in to their bosses' moods, the opposite is rarely the case. This can become especially problematic during economic downturns, when rumors of layoffs tend to fly. To keep your finger on the pulse, go for a walkabout, eat lunch in the cafeteria, and ask a few people you trust to tell you what they are picking up.

That's what Doug did after the 2008 financial crisis, when every day brought news of more layoffs, and fear and anxiety was at an all-time high in the American workplace. Campbell had promoted healthy lifestyles and walking in the workplace for years. To make sure he was tuned into what was going on, Doug took the practice to a new level. He bought himself a pair of sneakers and a pedometer and began to walk around the complex regularly, clocking ten thousand steps each day.

At first, people were surprised when the CEO showed up at the loading dock or stopped by their offices to say hello. But before long, they took advantage of these spontaneous TouchPoints to talk about what was on their minds. That allowed Doug to tune in and get a better feel for the mood; equally important, his calm demeanor sent a reassuring message throughout the company: "I'm here." "We're in this together." "We'll be OK."

FOLLOW THROUGH WITH SPEAKING

In a TouchPoint, you want to speak from your heart, so that people become engaged, and you need to speak from your head, so that what you say makes sense to them. Furthermore, you need to speak skillfully and exponentially, so that your message will be clearly understood through several degrees of separation.

Attending to all three is not easy, however. When we speak, we often assume that what we say is so clear that there is no chance of misunderstanding—after all, *we* know what we mean. It isn't until the message comes back to us changed or something doesn't happen the way we expected that we realize we had not been as clear as we thought we had. That's what happened to Doug.

Doug had a vision for the new Employee Center. He told the project team for the new building that he wanted the café to feature the world's best soup bar, a soup bar befitting the world's preeminent soup company. Then he turned his attention to other things. If it had not been for his accident, he would have followed up sooner, but it was a few months before he reconnected with the team to go over the plans. "Don't worry," they assured him, "the soup bar will be within budget."

Within budget? Doug thought. *Where did that come from?* To this day, he doesn't know exactly what happened. But it was probably a little like the proverbial telephone game where one person whispers a message into the ear of the next person in a circle, who whispers it to the next person, and so on. By the time the message reaches the first person again, it is unrecognizable.

Here's how Doug's message might have gotten changed. After he said to the project team that he wanted the world's best soup bar, one of the VPs might have told people over in the US Soup group that they needed "the world's best soup bar, but it has to be within budget." When the message was passed on again, it may have become "We need good-quality everything, but this is our budget." By the time the message got back to Doug, it had been transformed from "the world's best soup bar" to "a good soup bar within budget." At that point, Doug had to intervene, revise the budget, and do some last-minute scrambling. It wasn't that he didn't know how to be clear; it was just that he had not communicated the message so clearly and consistently that it reached everyone involved.

Speak from Your Head

As Doug's experience illustrates, one of the most important things to do in a TouchPoint is to clarify expectations. It seems like an easy thing to do, but all too often we forget. We assume people know what we mean, instead of checking to make sure they really got the message.

When a leader is not sufficiently clear, people fill in the gaps themselves. They decide what a "quality outcome" looks like, make assumptions about what "within a reasonable time" means, or figure out when and how to hold themselves accountable. If their assumptions are wrong, as assumptions often are, people may not meet your expectations, resulting in feelings of disappointment and frustration, wasted time, loss of confidence, and, sometimes, higher costs.

Speak from Your Heart

When you need to engage people on your issue, you need to make a strong personal connection. The more you are asking of them, the stronger the connection needs to be.

Andy, a VP of information technology who was leading a large-scale cost-savings project, needed to engage in thousands of TouchPoints to make the project a reality. He used to see work and the emotional side of life as separate (something he attributes to his British upbringing), but he had begun to realize that this viewpoint was limiting his effectiveness as a leader.

As he engaged in TouchPoints with senior executives, Andy decided to push himself beyond his natural inclination to have functional, task-oriented, programmatic interactions. Instead, he took the time to work on the relationships. He paid more attention to how the project was affecting people. He would say things like "We haven't got all the answers, but we know there is a great opportunity here" and "We're not sure if we will go in this direction yet, but we would really appreciate your input."

Uncharacteristically, Andy became more transparent and open about what the project meant for him, the organization, and everyone concerned. "It does take more time to build relationships, but it pays off. Because I was able to connect better, I got to where we were going faster. Also, instead of certain issues coming up later, we were able to deal with them up front."

When leading major change initiatives, one of the greatest challenges is to get people excited and committed to the change. To do so, you need to speak from your heart and share your enthusiasm for the project.

In the CEO Institute, one of our guest speakers is the executive coach Bob Gordon, who uses a particular drill to help people speak with emotion. It's a practice you can easily try with the help of a colleague and a copy of a classic speech like the Gettysburg address.

Begin by reading a few sentences of the speech to your colleague as if you were reading to a large audience. Then ask your colleague to stand a few feet away from you, and tell him that you are going to read the speech again with the intent to move him. Say, "Whenever my words touch you, move toward me. When they don't, move back." Then practice until you connect so consistently that the person ends up standing right next to you.

Once you've been able to do that with the classic speech, see if you can do it when talking about your own leadership model or a current project. As you become more comfortable speaking from your heart, you will make a much stronger connection in the moment. People will get a better sense of who you are and what you stand for, and they will be more likely to trust your intentions.

Speak Exponentially

In this interruption age, we engage in smaller and smaller TouchPoints, and in many more of them. Those brief interactions also travel faster and farther than ever before: a quick text message to a colleague in another building can make it around the world in seconds. Consequently, it has become imperative for leaders to master the power of exponential communication (listening and speaking), both face-to-face and in writing.

One of the ways Doug does this is by writing ten to twenty personal notes every day to thank people for their contributions, welcome new hires, or congratulate leaders on promotions or other successes. He writes the notes to individuals, who often share them with many other people. Over the years, these notes have added up to tens of thousands of TouchPoints. They energize those who receive them, such as the newly hired quality manager in Australia, who was amazed that the CEO not only knew she had joined the company but was happy to have her on board—and had taken the time to write a personal note to tell her so. And these TouchPoints send positive impulses all over the world.

Another way to put your ideas into wide circulation is to forget about the PowerPoint slides and tell more stories. That was one of the skills the executives at Pandora learned during a four-day workshop in New York. As Pandora was growing tremendously and adjusting to life after the IPO, uniting the long-term workforce with the many new employees through the company's core values became paramount. This required each executive not only to personally embody the values but also to be able to bring them to life by telling compelling stories. The executives made the values more vivid, and therefore more memorable, by encapsulating them in three distinct icons: the giraffe (great perspective and a big heart), the lion pride (individual competencies and intense teamwork), and the bumblebee (a beat-the-odds attitude). Each leader used these three symbols as a lead-in to a story about the values. The key was to tell a story that was so interesting that people could remember it and pass it on to others.

But speaking exponentially is not only about the words you use. It's also about actions, and when an entire executive team adopts the same practice, they can send a strong signal. That was the intention behind a small practice at YLE, the Finnish equivalent of Britain's BBC. For decades, the company had been structured so that the governing party of Finland could not unilaterally control the media. By design, the executive team was divided, and the directors formed competing factions. With the advent of digital media competition, however, YLE needed to move more quickly to continue to serve the Finnish public well, and that required a unified leadership team. But the team's composition had not changed, and the trust among directors was not high. Yet what was needed was for them to stand shoulder to shoulder facing the future, so that employees and other constituents could not continue to drive wedges between them to serve their partisan agendas.

Mette worked with the team during this transition. Once a quarter, she led a one-day off-site session during which the directors dealt with critical leadership issues. At the end of one such session, she gave them a seemingly small assignment: "Sometime during the next three months, invite three former 'opponents' to lunch in the large atrium cafeteria where everyone can see you." It was a small symbolic action, but it really got people's attention as they saw their directors breaking bread together.

LIFT YOUR GAME

The more difficult a TouchPoint and the higher the risk, the more skilled you need to be. For people to count on you in highly visible and highly sensitive situations, they need to trust both your intentions (that you will look out for the greater good) and your skills. To reach that level of competency requires intense practice.

K. Anders Ericsson, Michael J. Prietula, and Edward T. Cokely, authors of *The Cambridge Handbook of Expertise and Expert Performance*, emphasize that it takes incredible drive and tenacity to be among the best in your field. "The development of genuine expertise," they write, "requires struggle, sacrifice, and honest, often painful self-assessment. There are no shortcuts."[1] Their research shows that it takes about ten thousand hours of conscious and deliberate practice to become among the best in any domain.

How good are you? How skilled are you at communicating in a way that is tough-minded—giving clear

[1] K. Anders Ericsson, Michael J. Prietula, and Edward T Cokely, "The Making of an Expert," *Harvard Business Review*, July-August 2007, p. 2.

instructions, setting the pace, raising the bar, and holding people accountable? How good are you at communicating in a way that is tender-hearted—engaging people, understanding all sides, anticipating how your decisions impact others, and coaching others? You want to hone your skills so that whatever style is called for in the moment (directive or supportive, resolute or responsive), you can use it skillfully.

World-class performers practice intensely for about three hours a day to stay on top of their game. That is probably not realistic for you. But it is realistic to select one skill that you will practice during the coming week. For example, you might ration the number of times you allow yourself to speak during a meeting, or you might choose to listen so intently that you become brilliant at summarizing in just a few sentences what others say.

As you practice, don't worry about how good you are compared to your peers. Instead, focus on how good you are compared to how good you could become. Keep stretching yourself. Each time you push yourself in a TouchPoint, you will emerge a little stronger and a little more capable, with a little more confidence in your abilities as a leader.

You don't have to do it all on your own. To help the participants in the CEO Institute, we ask them to read Geoff Colvin's book *Talent Is Overrated: What Really Separates World-Class Performers from Everybody Else.*

They then work in small groups to help one another design a new practice that will be mentally demanding and a real stretch. They make commitments to help one another stick to their workouts, give one another frequent feedback, and track their progress. You can do the same by forming supportive relationships with colleagues or by working with a coach or mentor.

As Ed observed, leadership is hard! But whatever skills you need to develop, the key is to practice until you feel confident in your ability to handle whatever might be thrown at you in the moment. In turn, such confidence will allow you to be more open, more at ease, and more adaptable whenever you engage with others around an issue.

THE POINT IS . . .

Wynton Marsalis, director of the Lincoln Center Jazz Orchestra, considers a pristine technique to be a sign of morality. It is the way to see whether someone is serious. Not mastering the technique is, to him, like an athlete who comes to a game out of shape. "Don't start professing a love for the game. The love is what would have made you get your ass in shape."[2] To Marsalis, love is the spiritual essence of what we do. Technique is the way we tangibly demonstrate it.

[2]Wynton Marsalis, *To a Young Jazz Musician: Letters from the Road* (Random House, 2004), p. 62.

Whether you are a leading artist or a world-class leader, real learning requires both *passion* and *practice*. Yes, it is hard; it is also intensely rewarding.

Have you watched a child who is learning to read? The way she concentrates so completely that her tongue sticks out or her toes curl. The way she persists. And then, her sheer joy as she recognizes the letters, spells a word, reads a sentence, and, finally, reads a whole book. Her elation is contagious.

That joy is there for all of us when we push ourselves to the limit and slightly beyond. It is there when we make the commitment to practice.

6

Mastering the Touch

How Can I Help?

Having watched the president and CEO of Pandora, Mikkel Vendelin Olesen, in action, it was clear to Mette that he loved to lead. "If you had met me ten years ago," Mikkel told her, "you would have seen a different person. Back then I would run with the ball thinking, 'Look at me, look at me, look at me!'"

"What changed?" Mette asked.

Mikkel replied that after he was given more responsibility, he discovered that he loved to take poorly performing teams to a higher level. "Seeing people's potential and lifting them to a completely new level is a real kick," he said. "I guess when you have enough of your own medals in the cabinet, it simply becomes more satisfying to win them with others."

Every leader has his or her own unique style. But when it comes to mastering the touch, they all have one thing

123

in common. When dealing with others, they think less about what they can *get* and more about what they can *give*. They no longer ask what the organization can do for them, but look for ways they can serve the organization.

FOUR MAGIC WORDS: "HOW CAN I HELP?"

Leadership is not about *you*—it's about *them*. Whether the TouchPoint is about your issue, their issue, or an issue you share, asking (in your own mind or directly), "How can I help?" at the start of an interaction opens up space for people to voice their ideas, concerns, and viewpoints. Those four magic words shift the focus from what *you* want to communicate or accomplish to finding out what *they* want and need from you. In Doug's case, hearing those four words from Neil McKenna transformed his outplacement experience and ultimately his leadership philosophy.

To see the situation from the other people's point of view and be as helpful as you can, you need to not only use your head, your heart, and your hands; you also need to have the touch. That means you need to develop what in German is called *fingerspitzgefühl*, "fingertip sensitivity." When you have both the skills and the touch, you can read the situation, develop good timing, and calibrate your response using the right level of intensity.

Timing can be particularly important. Anne remembers an insight from earlier in her career when she was in charge of human resources and communication for a private equity firm. No matter who "owns" the issue, she said, you need to know *when* to address it. "If the person is having their moment of glory and being congratulated, that is *not* the time to go in and give corrective feedback, and certainly not in public."

Anne recalls sitting in on a presentation by a junior person. It went well, "But there were some rough edges. The easiest thing would have been to pull him aside right then or send a quick email right afterwards with seven things he could've done better. But I checked myself and thought about how I could best help him."

A couple of days later, Anne dropped into his office. "I started out talking about how proud the team must have felt to get to that stage in the project," she said. "Then, knowing he had five more opportunities to give the same presentation, I asked, 'What do you think is the one thing you want to work on? Can I help?'" They spent a little time discussing the one thing he mentioned and working through it together. "He felt in control and was clearly energized," Anne said. "He was happy, and that made me feel happy. And I knew the next presentation was going to be better."

THE TOUCHPOINT TRIAD

In music, a triad describes the three tones you need to form a complete chord, the three notes that create the harmony. Likewise, a TouchPoint triad describes the three

key notes you have to hit to be helpful in even the briefest
of moments.

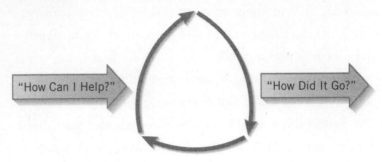

Asking the magic question, "How can I help?"
prepares you for the triad. The first note, listening
intently, helps you figure out what is really going on
and what others need from you; it is a way to tangibly
demonstrate that you care. The second note, framing the
issue, ensures that everyone in the TouchPoint has
the same understanding of the situation. The third note,
advancing the agenda, means deciding what next steps
to take and who will take them. After the TouchPoint is
over, following up with a question such as "How did it
go?" or "Is there anything else you need from me?" is
a reminder that you care; in addition, the other people's
response lets you know how things worked out and
whether you were genuinely helpful.

That's it! You move toward mastery by listening
intently, framing the issue, and advancing the agenda.
So as you engage in TouchPoint after TouchPoint,
all you need to remember is "listen-frame-advance,"

"listen-frame-advance." And you do it dozens of times each day, day after day.

The First Note: Listen Intently

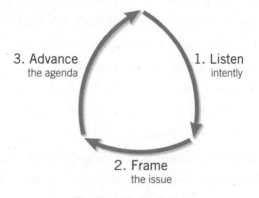

3. Advance
the agenda

1. Listen
intently

2. Frame
the issue

The TouchPoint Triad

Craig, the principal at a magnet school in Utah, has the process down pat. His office is a bit like Grand Central Station, with students and teachers constantly coming and going. All day long, Craig listens, clarifies expectations, and drives toward decisions, either by helping people make a call or doing it for them. People often are in and out of his office in ten minutes, even counting a little banter and horsing around. Yet his staff and students never feel rushed, because he always gives them his undivided attention for that time. When he doesn't have the time, he doesn't pretend to be available. He just says, "Not now; I am too busy." That's not a problem, because they know they will get the attention they need later on.

Even in the briefest TouchPoint, Craig hits each of the three key notes. He listens to help people get to the crux of the matter. Once he is sure that he and the others have the same understanding of the issue, he asks, "What is it you are really asking me to do? Do you want some advice, just to talk it through, or for me to make a decision?" If the issue doesn't seem clear enough, he may ask them to grab a marker and capture the salient points or list the options and capture the pros and cons. Depending on the relationship, the level of trust, and the other people's level of experience, he might keep quiet and just listen, letting them figure it out themselves. Sometimes he makes the decision about next steps, but when it is their issue, he tries to get them to make the call. Throughout the process, he keeps the focus on the school's mission by asking them, "What would be the best for the students?"

Like Craig, you have countless opportunities to perfect your touch. Just think about it. How many TouchPoints do you think you engage in every day? Most leaders say several dozen. Let's say you might have about seventy interactions each day, including casual hallway and phone conversations, discussions in Web-based meeting rooms, and quick exchanges of text. That adds up to twenty-five thousand opportunities in a year.

One reason Craig can get so much done in such brief TouchPoints is that he is an "aerobic listener"—he is present, pays attention, and tunes into the other people.

Careful listening lets you connect with the others, pick up nuances, zero in on the issue, figure out whose issue it is, and determine what kind of help people need.

Begin with a quick scan to find out whether you ought to engage fully and, if so, when and for how long. Ask yourself, What's the issue? What kind of help are they looking for from me? Whose issue is this—mine, theirs, or ours? What are the time limitations? Is the issue material to the business or a matter of principle (or both)? There are many demands on your time, and you need to invest your energy and attention where you can be most helpful and where it serves the team or organization the most.

Once you decide to engage fully, ask yourself, *What's really going on?* Be curious. Ask for the evidence—relevant objective data, such as numbers, tangible constraints, and deadlines. If there is only intangible evidence, try to get a sense of the magnitude by asking for a subjective 1–10 rating of the situation.

Keep listening for the real issue. Are there gaps in the information you are getting? If there is something you don't understand, say so. Listen to the people who are present and seek to understand other conversations that have led up to this one. Invest whatever time you need to make sure you fully grasp the issue, because when it concerns your area of responsibility, you want to understand it better than anyone else on the planet.

Finally, be intellectually honest about what is really going on. We all have a tendency to hear what we want to hear and listen for the data that confirm our preconceived opinions. It takes mental discipline to allow yourself to hear and understand what is *really* going on. Keep in mind that there is nothing as useless as solving the wrong problem. It may feel good to move quickly, but moving too fast only creates the illusion of progress and undermines your credibility as a leader.

As you listen, be sure also to tune into the other people's energy and their level of commitment. Is their energy red, yellow, or green? Does it shift during the conversation? If people arrive with green energy and it turns yellow during the TouchPoint, you are not really helping them. If, in contrast, they come in with their shoulders slumping and leave with a bounce in their step, you did something right.

The Second Note: Frame the Issue

Here's a situation that might sound familiar. You are in a meeting where remarks have been flying all over the room but nothing is happening. Then one person says, "It seems to me there are three things going on," and proceeds to summarize in just a few sentences everything that was said, adding, "Did I get this right?" or "Did I miss something?"

No matter what the person's position, he or she mastered the first note of the triad brilliantly by listening carefully enough to be able to pull out the essence of what people were trying to say. People probably felt relieved; there was a meeting of the minds, and they felt they were getting somewhere.

Before you move on to the second note in the triad, take a moment to summarize what you heard, to make sure you got it right. Then you will be ready to frame the issue in a way that can help the other people in the TouchPoint think about it more clearly. When you do that superbly, people will be able to explain it to others in a way that is clear and compelling.

Larry, vice president of international for a Fortune 500 company, did just that in a brief conversation with Chuck, the head of the consumer insights group. Chuck had been charged with helping put together a presentation for an analyst meeting. "This was a really big presentation and a very important one," Larry explained. "Chuck came into my office and asked, 'Where do I start?' I thought that what he needed to do was to focus on two things: honesty and hope."

Larry suggested to Chuck that he could talk frankly and openly about the things the company had done well, and just as frankly about the things that weren't working. He told Chuck, "What they want to know is, 'Do you get it?' Then give these guys a good reason to stay with us. Tell them, 'Yes, there are some problems, but here is what we are doing about it.'"

Once Larry framed the presentation with those two little words, *honesty* and *hope*, Chuck was good to go. He knew what to do next. As to follow-up? "I won't seek him out," Larry said, "because then it may seem like I own the issue. But when I run into him, I'll ask how it went." With those two words, Larry helped Chuck get clear about the issue. How you frame what you have heard depends partly on whether people need greater *clarity*, as Chuck did, or whether they need greater *confidence* or *commitment*.

If people need more *clarity*, you might have to roll up your sleeves and dive into the data with them. They might need some context to understand the competitive land-scape and the developments everyone should be watching more closely. Or they may need to understand how their work supports the company's top priorities, that is to say, a clear line of sight to the strategy. Sometimes you need to bring in models that are unique to your discipline, such as financial formulas, marketing matrices, or work-process flow charts. The key is to provide whatever people need to help them see things more clearly.

Sometimes people have difficulty focusing on the issue because they are struggling to choose among too many options: on the one hand, there is this; on the other hand, there is that; and if there were a third hand, they would bring that in as well. In that case, you need to help them sort through the options. The conversation might go something like this: "So it sounds like we can either do A or B, is that correct?" "Which do you think would be the best choice?" "Okay, if A is the best choice, then you are telling me that we have three options: 1, 2, or 3, right?"

"Well, which option do you prefer?" "Option 2? I agree. So since we both like option 2, what does that mean in terms of next steps?"

If the issue looks like one of *confidence* or *commitment*, think about what the people love to do and what they are good at. Connect their passion (what drives them) to the purpose of the project. Help them see why their strengths make them uniquely suited for handling it. If they are tired, you might go for a walk together or tell them to take the rest of the day off. If they are overwhelmed, help them define the problem or cut it down to a manageable size. If they seem complacent, talk about the gravity of the situation and stress the need to act with utmost urgency. Whatever the situation, you want to speak from your heart. Let people know *why* their contribution matters, and show that you have confidence in them.

The Third Note: Advance the Agenda

Remember, when people come to you with an issue, they want to make progress. Once you know what is needed, do what you can in that moment to move the agenda forward. If you need to help people make a decision or if you need to make the decision yourself, do it. If you need to connect them to someone, make a call or send an instant message. Show a bias for action.

For many people, the challenge when it comes to making decisions is that they are afraid they will make the wrong call. When that happens, remind people of the risk in *not* acting. Make it clear that no one makes the perfect decision every time; it's just not possible. All any of us can do is consider the information available at the moment, make the best decision we can, and move on.

Doreen, head of global IT services in a large firm, looked at it this way: "If you can move quickly and get it right eight or nine times out of ten, that's pretty good. When you don't get it right, you go back and fix it." When you are unencumbered by trying to be perfect, you are free to move faster. As Doreen would say, "I know I am going to be wrong sometimes, and if I am wrong, I know I am going to fix it."

That being said, having a bias for action doesn't mean that your decisions should be impulsive. When your actions could have serious consequences, it may be more risky to act than not to act. In fact, when it comes to substantive issues, the final decision is seldom made in any one meeting. Instead, it is the culmination of an elaborate sequence of TouchPoints in which minor advances were made all along the way.

That was the case when Samir (not his real name), a specialist with a global management consulting firm, concluded a three-month engagement with Justin. This was the last in a series of meetings about Justin's performance, and the most difficult one, because the latest assessment showed that Justin was still not performing up to par.

Samir sat down with Justin and framed the situation: "I know you feel the company owes you, because they asked you to transfer into this role, but the fact is that the results are just not there. The company made a mistake. So we have two options: you can go back to your previous role where you were a strong performer, or we can help you find a role outside the organization."

Justin argued that he deserved another chance, but the fact was that the three-month assessment had been his last chance. So Samir said, "Yes, you were brought over to this position, but it hasn't worked. How can I help you come to a decision?"

The problem many leaders have is that they try to do too much in any one interaction. Instead, loop back later. For pivotal decisions, such as getting rid of the barbed wire around the Campbell headquarters, it may take dozens of follow-up TouchPoints before the decision is implemented.

As you need to get the work done through shorter and more frequent bursts of interactions in this interruption age, the risk is that you may not go deep enough on some issues. Therefore, be sure to set aside significant chunks of time with your team members, collectively and individually, during which you can address the issues in a thorough and comprehensive way and prepare for what may lie ahead.

FOLLOW THROUGH: "HOW DID IT GO?"

Among other things, following up helps you learn how well you are doing at listening, framing the issue, and helping people move forward. For example, a good outcome suggests that you did well, whereas a negative one might indicate that what you thought was the issue was actually a symptom of something else. Or it could be that the thinking was clear, but the plan for how to move forward was flawed.

Following up also helps you find out whether the decision was executed properly and how well it is working. Unfortunately, most leaders are so busy that as soon as a TouchPoint is over, they are on to the next thing, getting back to the issue only when something is *not* working. But you want to loop back *before* there is a problem. So once decisions about next steps have been made and the Touch-Point is over, make a note to follow up either formally (your issue) or casually (their issue). This is not a checkup but a check-in, a tangible way to show that you care.

When other people own the issue, following up is also an opportunity to reinforce their confidence or simply to express appreciation. For example, you might stop by someone's office or send a note saying something like, "I'm really glad you brought up that issue. That kind of information will help us in setting next year's priorities."

Or "Thank you for bringing that to my attention. By getting ahead of this problem, we'll avoid what might have been an unpleasant surprise."

THE FOUR A'S OF AN EFFECTIVE TOUCHPOINT

Having the touch in a TouchPoint is not just about doing plant tours or coaching someone on her presentation. It is about really connecting, being present to the possibilities, advancing the agenda, and improving performance. It is about engaging in a way that is *alert, abundant, authentic,* and *adaptable.*

The Four A's of an Effective TouchPoint

The pianist Richard Goode embodies these four characteristics when he gives a master class, and it is an inspiration to watch him in action. He is irrepressible in his love for the music (authentic). Each session begins with a student performing a piece she has practiced, such as a Mozart piano sonata. As she plays, Goode listens to every note with complete attention (alert). When she is finished, he beams at her and explains what he enjoyed about her technique and interpretation.

After telling the student what he has appreciated, Goode explains why he might take a different approach in some passages, pointing out interesting tensions in the piece and describing how he would resolve them (abundant). To help the student understand, he will talk, tap, hum, play a passage, and ask the student to try it (adaptable). Goode is so intent on helping that every student responds; you can watch people grow right before your eyes.

Imagine what you could achieve if you were to engage that way in at least a handful of TouchPoints every day. Think about how you might do that as we take a closer look at each of the four A's.

Alert

Being alert is about developing great situation sensing. Richard Goode is not only alert to the performance but also sensitive to how difficult it is for the student to be coached in front of an audience. As a leader, you can be so alert that you become superb at identifying the real issue. When you are fully present, you can see the gaps in someone's line of logic and pick up bits of information that provide clues to what is going on.

Doug honed his situational awareness when he helped put himself through graduate school by teaching tennis.

"The focus you had to bring to it was intense. During my free time, I would teach private lessons to as many as twenty people in a day, including macho men, six-year-olds, businesswomen, and grandparents. Session after session, I had to pay incredibly close attention to what they wanted to learn and what they were capable of doing, and then I had to give them such a good experience that they would want to come back again."

Abundant

To think in a way that is abundant, you need to reject the scarcity mind-set that says, "I can either hit the targets this quarter *or* build the capacity to deliver long term," and instead find ways to "get the job done now *and* next time." Instead of thinking "I can either be tough-minded *or* tender-hearted," you can be "tough on standards *and* enthusiastic about people."

Remember the story of RCMP superintendent Ward Clapham in Chapter Two? Ward always thinks "prepare *and* repair," and one of his greatest passions is keeping teenagers from getting into trouble with the law. The problem was that most officers talked to teenagers only when they had done something wrong, so it was hard to connect with them.

Ward came up with an initiative whereby police officers tried to catch kids doing good things and reward them with a "positive ticket." In the course of a year, his officers handed out forty thousand positive tickets, a 3:1 ratio compared to violations. As a result of that and other prevention initiatives aimed at young people, youth-related service calls dropped by almost 50 percent. That meant that more than one thousand at-risk youths stayed out of trouble.

Authentic

Lisa, the innovation team leader mentioned in Chapter One, observed, "There's a difference between having a job as a leader and authentically embracing what it means to be a leader. When I realized that I didn't need to fit some prescribed mold and just needed to be my best, it was incredibly freeing." As Lisa felt more comfortable about who she was as a leader, she let others see not only where she was strong but also where she was vulnerable. "It took a lot to do so, but by being more open, I was able to build better relationships. People really appreciated me showing more of myself. One person said, 'Now I know what your genuine intent is.'"

Being authentic means that leading is not just your job; it is your passion. If it is something you love to do, you will spend a lot of time thinking about it and becoming really good at it, which will make you love it even more. As you share your enthusiasm for leadership with others, they will *want* to join you. But being authentic also comes with a certain level of authority, because it means you will live by a very clear code that provides an underlying clarity and consistency in every TouchPoint.

As often happens, when Nancy, the newly promoted VP we mentioned in Chapter One, became clearer about her code, she became more courageous. "You have to stand up for the things you think are right." In the past, when she got pushback, she would let the matter go, even when she knew that her solution was the best one. "Now I stand up for what I believe. If there is too much tension in the moment, I won't grind on it. Instead I'll leave it for a bit, and then come back to it and approach it differently later. But I will be persistent."

Adaptable

The secret to being adaptable is to develop a broad range of skills, so that you can adjust and adapt in the moment. Does the situation require you to be directive ("Do as I say"), consultative ("What do you think?"), or inspiring ("We are changing the world")? Do you need to push people or be patient? Show strength or share a vulnerability? Step forward and take charge, or fall back so that someone else can take the lead? Whatever you do, the key is to do it skillfully.

Rita, a specialist in health care accreditation, exemplifies what it means to be adaptable. In her position, Rita needs to deliver results without the benefit of having formal authority. She recalls a particularly sensitive

TouchPoint she experienced with eight medical chiefs of staff who had to develop and commit to a common set of standards. Before the meeting, some of them had called her, expressing their concern about who would have the power to make decisions.

"At the beginning, the situation was tense," Rita recalls, "and I needed to really dig into my treasure chest of competencies to make the meeting a success." She used humor, provided clarity, deferred to the chiefs of staffs as the experts, asked precise questions, and offered ideas.

The meeting went so well and was so productive that, as the doctors were leaving, they were clearly elated. Realizing how difficult it had been to bring the group together, one of them even suggested that Rita had a future in diplomacy.

HOW CAN I DO BETTER TOMORROW?

"You learn a whole lot more from the things that didn't work than from the things that did work," says Larry. "Whenever we find things that don't work, the first thing I say is, 'What have we learned?' First order of business is learning from it, and, hopefully, ensuring that you don't make the same mistake again."

You know what it feels like when you have touched someone in a positive way, because she is a little clearer, a little more confident, or a little more committed to going forward. Even better, you know she will take that energy with her to future interactions, lighting up the organization's synapses along the way.

Conversely, you also know what it feels like when you blow it. It may be a little thing, yet it's as irritating as a pebble in your shoe. It could be something as trivial as having interrupted the exchange of pleasantries at the beginning of a phone conference. The minute you do it, you know your timing is off. If you had let the chit-chat continue for another minute or two, you could have moved on naturally to the issue.

At other times, however, you make mistakes with something more significant. That happened to Doug a few years ago when he made the decision to let a key team member go. For a variety of very good reasons, Doug had been advised not to give the person advance notice. Afterwards, he felt he had blindsided the person and not brought the appropriate level of compassion and respect to the relationship. "I was very conflicted through the whole thing," he said, "and in hindsight I should have had an ongoing dialogue with the individual, leading up to the final conversation. I could have made the process much more thoughtful and transparent."

He couldn't undo what he had done, but he could learn from it and do much better the next time. He still listens to other people's counsel when he has to handle a difficult situation, but ultimately he relies more fully on his own judgment.

When you do mess up—and you will—the key is to course-correct and to do it quickly. Remember the story of Ed and Carol in Chapter Five? When Ed lost his patience with Carol for her lack of progress on the company's growth plan, he apologized right away and told her that she should expect more of him. What is interesting is that such incidents often lead to a much stronger relationship in the future, as was the case with Ed and Carol. People will forgive you for messing up, as long as they can see that you are doing your best to improve.

If you really want to make progress, do your own "post-game analysis" of your TouchPoints at the end of each day. Reflect on the dozens of connections you have made. Ask yourself, *What worked? What didn't? How can I do better?*

The leaders from the CEO Institute each do this in his or her own way. For example, one clears his calendar for the last hour of the day so that he has time to reflect before leaving the office. Another turns off the phone and radio during her commute home so that she can replay the day's events in her mind's eye. A third thinks about the day's TouchPoints when he is walking the dog at night.

This is the practice of doing a little better tomorrow than you did today, so that you can constantly increase the ratio of "That went well" to "I blew it." This is about not only *getting* experience but, more important, *learning* from your experience. If a TouchPoint went badly, ask yourself why. Was your leadership model not working as you anticipated? Did you become defensive because of something that was said? Were your skills not up to par? When you do mess up, remember that the most powerful thing you can do is acknowledge your mistake, commit to do better, and make sure you follow through. Say, "I'm sorry; I dropped the ball. I'll get back to you on this." And then do it!

As you think about what worked and what didn't, it is a great idea to capture your insights in a leadership journal. That way, you can periodically review what you have learned and detect the patterns. The fact is, most leaders struggle with the same problems over and over again throughout their careers, and it takes a concerted effort to break the pattern. Seeing the problem in black and white can help you find the discipline to do something about it.

The ongoing discipline of inquiry, reflection, and practice will help you become an ever better leader. And there will always be more to learn. For example, once you perfect your skills in the TouchPoint, the challenge becomes how to be more consistent. And when you become more consistent, the next challenge is to develop the leaders around you so that they too can become more effective.

THE POINT IS . . .

Visions and strategies are merely promises. The job of a leader is to translate those promises into real, on-the-ground performance. But how do you take abstract concepts and ground them in reality? How do you take inanimate bullet points and infuse them with life? You do it one TouchPoint at a time.

As Irene (Chapter Two) observes, you can't fly in on a helicopter and yell, "Hey, roll out that strategy! Make that target!" In her experience, "Leadership is all about gardening. The care and feeding, the watering and fertilizing, and you need to do it every day. And you also need to prune and pluck out the weeds, because if you leave the garden untended, it goes to hell." You need to be tough and tender as you grow people and improve their performance.

Your workdays are filled with planned and impromptu meetings, long emails and short messages, videoconferences and major events. One TouchPoint at a time, you achieve a meeting of the minds and a coordination of efforts. You listen to objections and look for solutions. You come in earlier, deal with problems faster, and buy ice cream for everyone. You stay engaged until each person stops doing the old behaviors and starts adopting new ones.

Each day, you look for ways to be helpful. Andrew, VP of a multibillion-dollar division, states the challenge this way: "I prefer to help in the areas where I'm naturally strong, such as conceptual thinking skills and problem solving. What is harder for me is inspirational leadership, but people need both. On a day-to-day basis, you need to inspire confidence and generate a feeling of optimism. You need them to feel 'I want to go with this person.'"

To remind himself of the importance of inspiring others, Andrew keeps this notion front and center by writing it on the whiteboard in his office. His message to himself reads: "I coach daily—I understand their objectives—How can I help today?—What would be a good outcome?" Thanks to this approach, Andrew has been able to deliver strong results, and, he says, "It has helped me a lot personally. I'm even a much better father because of it."

The leadership literature talks a great deal about the crucible moments that mold your character. Yet it is the millions of ordinary, everyday moments that ultimate shape your reputation. Mastering those begins with one simple question: "How can I help?"

Coda

*L*eadership is hard. The pressures are mounting, the complexities are escalating, the demands are never-ending, and even if you were to work 24/7, you could never get everything done. That is just the way it is.

Yet no matter how hard it can be to achieve ever higher levels of performance, we believe you can approach each day with a sense of optimism and focus your energy on the things you can control. When you are clear-headed and clear-hearted, you can consistently direct your attention to *the issues* that are material to the business, a matter of principle, or both. When you are clearly competent, you can engage *the other people* in a way that increases their commitment and confidence.

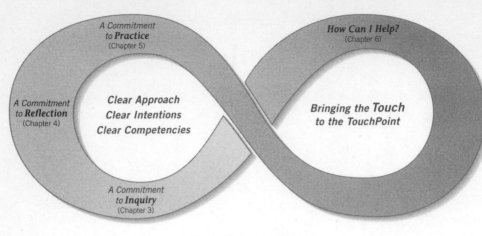

A Commitment to Mastery

And you can start today. The beauty of TouchPoints is that they are both approachable and aspirational: every moment is an opportunity to *aim* for mastery, while *achieving* mastery will remain an elusive target. That's because mastery is not a destination—it's a quest. It is a commitment to developing ever greater clarity and capabilities so that you may become ever more helpful in the moment.

By concentrating your energy and attention on the things you can control, you will become the type of leader whom others count on to meet the targets, raise the standards, and exceed the performance expectations. As your reputation grows, you will be trusted with even greater responsibilities. That will require you to push yourself to even deeper levels of inquiry, reflection, and practice. As you do, you will improve your capacity to lead wisely (efficiently and sustainably) in the interruption age.

We encourage you to embark on this journey with a sense of both realism and optimism. There is a Touch-Point right around the corner. Use it well.

Recommended Reading

These are the texts the participants in Campbell's CEO Institute are asked to read. You can find a list of Doug's favorite books at www.ConantLeadership.com and a list of Mette's at www.MetteNorgaard.com.

Jim Collins, "Level 5 Leadership," *Harvard Business Review*, July-August 2005

Geoffrey Colvin, *Talent Is Overrated* (Portfolio, 2008)

Stephen R. Covey, *The 7 Habits of Highly Effective People* (Simon & Schuster, 1989)

Bill George, *Authentic Leadership* (Jossey-Bass, 2003)

Marshall Goldsmith, *What Got You Here Won't Get You There* (Hyperion, 2007)

Jon R. Katzenbach, *Teams at the Top* (Harvard Business Press, 1998)

Jim Loehr and Tony Schwartz, *The Power of Full Engagement*
(Simon & Schuster, 2003)

Dan Roam, *The Back of the Napkin* (Portfolio, 2009)

Meg Wheatley and Myron Kellner-Rogers, *A Simpler Way*
(Berrett-Koehler, 1996)

Acknowledgments

We thank our friends at Jossey-Bass for helping us bring this work to life. In particular, we are grateful to Susan Williams and Byron Schneider for guiding the completion of the project and to Warren Bennis for his endorsement of the work. We also appreciate the thoughtful discipline that Janis Chan brought to the writing of the final manuscript. Additional thanks go to John Hoover for helping us find the "spine" of our idea and to Bill George for helping us connect with Jossey-Bass.

A special acknowledgment goes to the staff and participants of the Campbell Soup Company CEO Institute, who helped us shape our thinking over the past five years. Their spirited approach to learning and growing as leaders both inspired and humbled us. We are particularly grateful to Nancy Reardon, Mary Lemonis, Elizabeth Walker, and Fran Bruno for helping us realize the full potential of the CEO Institute itself. We also thank our friends at

FranklinCovey for bringing us together many years ago at a leadership retreat in Sundance, Utah. In particular, we acknowledge Stephen R. Covey, Stephen M. R. Covey, Greg Link, Craig Pace, and our late friend Blaine Lee for their encouragement over the years.

On a more personal note, Mette thanks her clients, especially the leaders who shared their stories and insights for this book. It is their responsibilities, their ambitions, and their challenges that inspire her to search for new and better ways to lead. She also thanks the colleagues who gave thoughtful feedback on early versions of the manuscript, and the friends who were always there when she needed their advice or support: Else Relster, Laurie Julian, Craig Pace, Rita Pedersen, Dorthe Nørgaard, Anette Steenberg Williams, and Olli-Pekka Heinonen.

Mette is deeply indebted to Flemming Flyvholm, her good friend and writing coach extraordinaire. His guidance, insights, and encouragement were invaluable. Most of all, Mette is grateful to her husband, Alfredo Sánchez Gómez, for his unwavering support during the years it took to write this book, and especially for the countless conversations that helped her explore the nuances of every idea and strengthen the line of logic. He also reviewed every draft, scrutinized the punctuation, and cooked dinner. Alfredo is a true partner in business, in learning, and in life.

Doug first acknowledges his wife, life partner, and best friend, Leigh. Her steadfast love, counsel, and support have been invaluable to his journey as a husband, a father, a friend, a colleague, and a leader. Also, his children, Ben, Tyler, and Sarah, have been a constant source of pride and inspiration. His parents, Roger and Elsie, created a wonderfully solid platform for his growth and development, a platform that has been continually enhanced by his larger extended family, both related and beyond. He is particularly appreciative of the steadfast support of his friends Bruce Lipstein and Jim Mead.

A multitude of corporate leaders over the past thirty-five years have influenced Doug's thinking and personal growth. Three for whom he worked for extended periods of time stand out: Jim Kilts, H. John Greeniaus, and Harvey Golub. Doug is indebted to each of them for their tough-minded approach to the pursuit of excellence at work and their caring support of him as a person. He is also indebted to all of his friends and colleagues at Campbell Soup Company for their passionate, inspiring, and integrity-laden pursuit of excellence in the workplace, the marketplace, and the broader community. Together, in his opinion, they have begun to build the world's most extraordinary food company. Finally, he extends his deep thanks to his late friend and mentor, Neil McKenna, who helped him begin to see beyond his own agenda and to find the true meaning of "How can I help?"

In closing, we celebrate the provocative collaboration we experienced working together on this project. Although we clearly share an abiding interest in the study of leadership and the human condition, as well as common values and principles in our approach to life, we each bring very different life experiences to the work. Mette was born and raised in rural Denmark and has dedicated most of her professional life to helping organizations reach their full potential from the "outside in" as a sought-after thought leader, consultant, and executive coach. Doug was born and raised in the suburbs of Chicago, and has dedicated his professional life to helping organizations reach their full potential from the "inside out" as a corporate executive. We believe these different perspectives have stretched the thinking in this work in a very unique, rich, and well-rounded fashion. We have found ourselves enjoying these differences and delighting in the learning. We hope you do, too.

About the Authors

Douglas Conant was appointed president and chief executive officer of the Campbell Soup Company in 2001. He also was elected a director of the company at that time. Conant is the eleventh leader in this iconic company's 141-year history.

Under Conant's leadership, Campbell has reversed a precipitous decline in market value and employee engagement. The company has made significant investments to improve product quality and packaging, strengthen the effectiveness of its marketing programs, and develop a robust innovation pipeline. Campbell also has improved its financial profile, enhanced its relationships with its customers, and consistently improved its employee engagement through investments in its organization.

Over the past six years, Campbell has delivered cumulative total shareholder returns in the top tier of the global food industry and has achieved world-class employee engagement levels. As a result, the company has made substantial progress toward achieving its mission of building the world's most extraordinary food company by nourishing people's lives everywhere, every day. The company has been recognized for its progress, with honors including the 2010 Catalyst Award for helping women develop and advance their careers.

Conant joined Campbell with twenty-five years of extensive food industry experience from three of the world's leading food companies: General Mills, Kraft, and Nabisco. He began his career in 1976 in marketing at General Mills. After ten years, he then moved to Kraft, where he held top management positions in marketing and strategy. Immediately prior to coming to Campbell, he was president of the $3.5 billion Nabisco Foods Company, where he led that unit to five consecutive years of double-digit earnings growth.

A native of Chicago, Conant earned his BA degree from Northwestern University and his master's degree in business administration from the J. L. Kellogg School of Management at Northwestern.

Conant is incoming chairman of the Committee Encouraging Corporate Philanthropy (CECP) and a trustee of the International Tennis Hall of Fame in Newport, Rhode Island. He is past chairman and trustee of the Conference Board and is an active member and past chairman of the board of directors of the Grocery Manufacturers Association (GMA) as well as the nonprofit organization Students in Free Enterprise (SIFE). He is also a member of the board of directors of Catalyst.

To bring Conant to your organization and to access resources designed to help you start mastering your TouchPoints, visit www.conantleadership.com.

Mette Norgaard, PhD, MBA, an expert on strategic leadership and learning, works with executives and their teams to design and deliver culture-specific learning solutions that advance their strategies. Clients have included Microsoft, Metro International, Campbell Soup Company, Pandora, Finnish Broadcasting, and many others. She has also designed and participated in executive dialogues with thought leaders such as Stephen Covey, Jim Collins, John Katzenbach, Rob Goffee, Margaret Wheatley, and Ram Charan.

Client engagements have ranged from keynote presentations and multiday workshops to two-year programs. Assignments have frequently involved developing high-potential leaders, increasing employee engagement and initiative, and strengthening executive team dynamics. Examples of the latter are the transition to a new president, the evolution from an entrepreneurial culture to a more professional one, and the merger of two leadership teams.

Some solutions for executive teams were structured around quarterly huddles where the executives reflected on their behaviors over the previous three months and committed to improvements for the next quarter. Others have involved off-site sessions, each with a special focus (such as "the Head," "the Heart," and "the Hands"). A few have been one-of-a-kind leadership experiences, such as a recent one-year leadership journey that took an executive team to Thailand for the reflective work, to South Africa for a leadership safari and the study of natural efficiencies, and to New York City for an exploration of the collision of cultures and ideas.

For individual leaders, Norgaard has also served as a sparring partner to develop their personal leadership models. This work was done in one-to-one coaching sessions, with New York City as their learning laboratory.

Prior to starting her own practice, Norgaard worked with FranklinCovey Co. for ten years. As director of Covey Leadership Week, an executive retreat at Sundance, Utah, she taught executives from all over the world and from organizations such as Procter & Gamble, Johnson & Johnson, GE Capital, Estée Lauder, Harley-Davidson, Hard Rock Cafe, the U.S. Marine Corp, and the Royal Canadian Mounted Police. Norgaard was also part of a small group of consultants who led large-scale change processes for Fortune 500 firms and the U.S. government.

Norgaard is the author of the international best-seller *The Ugly Duckling Goes to Work* (Amacom, 2005), which has been translated into eight languages.

A native of Denmark, she lives with her husband in New York City.

To create leadership and learning solutions that will advance your organization's strategy, go to www.MetteNorgaard.com.

Index